Even Mountains Vanish

Even Mountains Vanish

Searching for Solace in an Age of Extinction

S u e E l l e n   C a m p b e l l

The University of Utah Press

Salt Lake City

The Defiance House Man colophon is a registered trademark of
The University of Utah Press. It is based upon a four-foot-tall
Ancient Puebloan pictograph (late PIII) near Glen Canyon, Utah.

Drawings of the sandhill crane for "The Voice of the Crane," the white-
tailed ptarmigan for "The Edge of Winter," the red-throated loon for
"String Games," and the northern oriole nest for "The World Is a Nest"
by SueEllen Campbell and Sherry Pomering.

Printed on acid-free paper
08 07 06 05 04 03
5 4 3 2 1

LIBRARY OF CONGRESS CALTALOGING-IN-PUBLICATION DATA

Campbell, SueEllen
   Even mountains vanish : searchng for solace in an age of extinction /
SueEllen Campbell
      p. cm.
ISBN 0-87480-771-9 (pbk. : alk. paper)
1. Natural history—Colorado. 2. Natural history—New Mexico.
3. Natural history—Canada, Northern. 4. Campbell, SueEllen. I. Title
QH105.C6 C26 2003
   508.7—dc21
                                                        2003010945

for John

Contents

Prologue

I stand at my kitchen counter with a bamboo brush in my hand. My grip is loose, my fingers just at the end of the handle, and I can feel the weight tip away from me. Propped between coffeepot and toaster oven is a pale gray piece of paper framed in black cardboard. I dip the bristles in a small glass box of water, then stroke brush against paper.

I start at the bottom left, move towards the center, level out with a small scoop, slide down to the bottom right. From the scoop, a light spiral up and to the side. Volcano, a breeze. There's magic in this paper, something that seems to transform water into black ink, but only for the minute or two it takes to evaporate.

I step back and watch as the volcano vanishes.

I dip my brush again. One long line left to right, thinning and thickening for beak, head, neck, body, legs, feet. Two broad bent strokes up from the body. Crane, flying. Beneath it I shape a butte, its downward slope echoing the curve from the bird's neck to chest. Bird and butte fade away.

Three arcs as round as I can make them, head, left side, right side, a quick scallop for a tail. I hold the brush closer to the bristles and carefully lay in a thick curved black beak, a round black eye. Already the body is growing faint, and soon only the eye and beak remain. Ptarmigan, winter plumage, in snow.

The things of this world float up through my memory, take form through my hand. An oriole nest, pendant. The curving chain of a backbone. A cluster of horsetails, jointed like bamboo. Jagged peaks. A marmot curled in a warm circle of repose. Low hills over water. Shooting star. A full moon rising.

I create each vision with a few lines, then watch it thin, pale, dissolve. Often a likeness sharpens as it dissipates, the angle of a wing or curve of a landscape revealing itself to be some kind of essential gesture. I can't control or predict this process, I can't freeze it at some perfect moment, but I am learning from watching how to make my own strokes spare and sure.

This painting is an exercise in loss and grief, a meditation on impermanence and letting go. Real volcanoes erode into nothing; real birds fly off into extinction. But it is also a space for creation, for imagination, wonder, and mystery. Here, what has gone may reappear. Over and over, birds soar across this sky, and mountains rise again.

I dip the brush once more. A crane dances from my hand.

Even Mountains Vanish

I

The Voice of the Crane

We had driven in earlier that afternoon across the Pajarito Plateau, past the bold signs for Los Alamos and into Bandelier National Monument, where we'd stopped at the rim of Frijoles Canyon to have our sandwiches in the sun. We'd been talking about our last visit a few winters before, when we had hiked down a deserted hanging trail to the Rio Grande. To our surprise, the river was frozen, and we sat alone on the rocky bank admiring the complicated textures of the ice, its turquoise gleams and shadows. Steller's jays flew about calling brightly, their cobalt feathers brilliant in the slanted light, and the ice creaked and sighed. Calm air and water, the world asleep under winter's white weight: in that tranquil and lovely place, it seemed, we could rest ourselves in a moment out of time. We'd remembered that serenity, and now, on this warm day in February, we had returned hoping for more.

So when we'd finished our lunch and my husband had wandered off to explore, I found a smooth spot on the ground, rolled my jacket into a pillow, and stretched out on my back.

The air felt cool and clean, the sun warm against my skin, my every breath was fragrant with piñon and juniper, and a pair of jays above me flashed like blue coal against the sky. I lay still, tried to stop the clatter of voices in my head, and waited for that infrequent but familiar feeling that some space inside me was opening up, making room for a kind of peace.

Usually I could bring on this transformation without much trouble, given a little time to myself in a quiet place outdoors, especially where the natural world seemed healthy. Even here, where the protected ruins and wilderness lands of the national monument lie immediately next to Los Alamos National Laboratory, I'd always been able to close my mind to things I didn't want to think about, put aside distress and let beauty in. Driving by the laboratory, I'd think for a few uneasy minutes about the irony of its location, how the top-secret home of the first nuclear bomb had been hidden so close above this placid canyon with its long-abandoned cliff houses and kivas. I'd offer a kind of ritual grimace, and then, the way I might shake loose from the sight of a highway crash, I'd turn my thoughts to the simpler scenes ahead.

Not today, though. Since my last visit here, the fifty-year anniversary of Hiroshima had passed. I'd been reading about the history of nuclear bombs and about radioactive contamination in the West. And I'd been typing my father's autobiography, learning about the time he spent during World War II as a cryptographer in the Pacific. I knew just enough more now to feel confused, just enough that I couldn't clear my mind.

So I lay brooding about aggression and fear, territoriality and defensiveness, creation and catastrophe. I thought about how the ancestral Puebloan people we often call the Anasazi had built their lives all across this part of the continent, stayed for centuries, then moved on for reasons we'll never know for certain, maybe pushed out by drought, by internal warfare, by violent invaders, how the people of this canyon and plateau might simply have moved nearby to today's Cochiti and San Ildefonso Pueblos, as their inhabitants believe. These small houses carved into high, inaccessible cliffs, then left empty for time and weather: what terrors might they have sheltered, what protections offered and lost?

I wondered about what might be buried in the volcanic soil under my back. Obsidian lance points ten thousand years old, relics of killings long forgotten? The traces of my own culture's weapons, lost bits of plutonium or uranium, hot pools or messy dumps of radioactive wastes, stray poisonous particles moving invisibly from earth to grass to deer? I imagined my father on Iwo Jima, a kid from Kansas swimming in the ocean around that wrecked island, encrypting and decrypting messages about the movements of B-29 bombers, while on this sunny plateau in northern New Mexico, scientists devised the bombs that would send him home to meet and marry my mother.

Was this just the same old sad story, the one about human violence, the endless damage we do, may always have done, to ourselves, each other, everything around us? Yes, I thought, but that didn't make it simple. I couldn't even tell myself that if humans are violent and destructive, the natural world, at least, is peaceful and enduring, not while I lay with my back pressed tightly against the remnants of enormous volcanic explosions and the cold winter earth stole my own body's warmth.

The longer I thought, the more confused I became. With every loop and tangle, the ironies grew more complex and elusive, the resonances more unsettling.

And yet this afternoon was too lovely for such dark brood-
ings, the sky too blue for a heavy heart, and a pair of golden
eagles had appeared above me, floating in big, easy circles, tug-
ging me back into the sunny present. I pulled my small binoculars from their case and fiddled with the focus until I could see
the shapes of the eagles' heads.

"What's that sound?" John asked, suddenly back beside me.
"Cranes!"

"No, it's still winter. It can't be."

But it was, that unmistakable gargle of sandhill cranes flying high overhead, higher than the eagles, moving north along
the Rio Grande for their age-old spring stopover in the
marshes of southern Colorado.

The sun poured through their long, narrow wings, first the
warm color of ripe wheat, then a flash of white or charcoal as
they angled and curved. They moved in a long, wavering V,
until a score or so would break loose, arc sideways, and spiral
back, brightening and darkening against the steady light.

Later in the afternoon we walked along the trail at the
bottom of Frijoles Canyon. The air was chilly in the shade of
the ponderosa pines, and we stepped carefully, for the patches
of ice were doubly slick with the day's melting. The great wall
to the north glowed like soft gold, and high above the mirror-
ing creek, the crumbling front walls of ancient houses echoed
the curves and angles of erosion. I stopped to read each inter-
pretive sign. One explained how the houses had been carved
with the sharp edges of basalt into the softer tuff of the cliffs
and plateau. What a lovely idea, I thought, to make a home in
a volcano with tools from a volcano. I leaned forward into the
flaky cinnamon-colored plates of bark on a ponderosa, pressed

my nose into one of the deeper crevices, and breathed in its warm vanilla scent.

A squirrel chattered up ahead, and I heard the short chip of a chickadee as I read another sign. We were standing in an ecotone, it said, a transition zone, where members of different biological communities mingle. I looked around. Narrow-leaf cottonwoods along the creek; the odd little horsetails that in summer would flourish along the damp banks like miniature groves of green bamboo; tall ponderosas here on the canyon's shady side, where the snow stays longest; curly-leafed Gambel oak with its bitter, nourishing acorns. A few other tourists passed by, one group speaking with British accents, another in German, a third in something that sounded to me like Russian.

I felt bombarded by messages. Everything around me was telling me something important, it seemed, but what?

I studied the pine needles strewn on the trail. Some were frozen into the ice, but others were loose, and I picked one up to feel its textures, its three long needles bound by a dark knot at one end. It was still flexible, and I began to braid its strands together as I walked. Piles of scat, greenish gray and full of white fur, announced the presence of coyotes, and the cutoff brushy ends of pine branches lay scattered at random, a sign of squirrels feeding on the trees' inner bark. A raven glided along the cliff top without once moving its wings.

Then another filament of cranes slid across the narrow slice of sky. Their strange music opened up the silence, that ancient and enigmatic gargling, and listening to them in the still winter day, I saw for an instant how much was happening here.

Above me birds were floating on thermals and migrating along invisible paths. The fallen cones of the ponderosas were expanding and popping, their seeds preparing to send out tendrils, and the leaves of oaks and cottonwoods were darkening into soil. Coyotes, foxes, mountain lions, all were sleeping somewhere not far away. Above me on the plateau, hidden caches of radioactive elements were throwing out their particles and rays. The cliffs I looked at, the crumbling yellow cups of houses, and the ground beneath my feet were eroding under water and ice, the mountains were melting, even the plate holding the continent was edging north and west, and the planet was spinning through space at an ungraspable speed—all as I meandered along the trail, in and out of the chilly shade, thinking my human thoughts.

Maybe this was all about time, all this afternoon's cryptic messages, my murmuring uneasiness, about how long things last, and in what forms. I knew so little of the history of this place—that Los Alamos National Laboratory had been here half a century, the cliff houses seven or eight centuries, humans a hundred centuries. The cranes had come earlier, certainly, but how much? Before these mountains, maybe even before the continents and oceans had taken their familiar places? I'd read on another sign that all this earth had emerged from the Jemez volcano in two great waves of eruptions, 1.1 and 1.4 million years ago. I knew this wasn't long in geological or evolutionary terms, but such numbers meant nothing real to me. I had no sense of their scale, no context for even beginning to understand them. And the other creatures around me, the ponderosas and horsetails, the fat dark Abert's squirrel that just now ran up the trail and stopped not four feet in front of us, with its huge tail, long black ear tufts, and an expression, it seemed, of hope—how old were these species? For how many centuries had they lived here, in this place?

Maybe I could learn the answers to some of these questions.

Then maybe I could begin to understand this scene, this afternoon in this place, hold its actors together in my mind in some proper proportion—the present and many pasts, sudden cataclysms and the peace of winter waters, atomic bombs and sandhill cranes.

The needles I'd been braiding together in my hands sprang apart.

The next day we drove home to northern Colorado, where John and I live in a red-rock-rimmed valley tucked between the Rocky Mountains and the Great Plains. Before we'd finished unloading the car, I was swept back into the demands and rhythms of my ordinary life: teaching literature and writing at Colorado State University, checking the page proofs of a book I'd recently finished, researching for an article I'd promised to write. I cooked and kept house, spent time with my parents in Denver. Around the edges of my days, I played with Marmot and Weasel, our two miniature dachshund puppies, and tried, without much success, to teach them to *come* and *sit* and *shhh* and *be nice to your brother.* Time for brooding was scarce, time for following my curiosity even scarcer, and the questions I'd started pondering during that afternoon in New Mexico receded into the background.

But they didn't disappear. A year passed, then a second spring, and I was still thinking about those questions. Though I didn't know why, I still felt haunted by all that I hadn't understood that day, the messages I'd sensed just beyond the range of my hearing or sight. I did know I wanted a way to think about that place that went beyond the simple contrasts between weapons laboratory and wilderness area, between violence and peace, human destructiveness and natural beauty. I suppose I also hoped for a richer context, a longer time scale, a broader stage, some unknown framework that might allow me to step back from, maybe even move beyond, the familiar, depressing recognition that I lived in a world of wounds, most of which I could do nothing at all to heal.

So when my schedule finally opened up, I decided to do a little research. I'd focus on this single place, the Pajarito Plateau, Frijoles Canyon, the Jemez volcano, and I'd find out its geological history. I'd look for the evolutionary ages of Abert's squirrels, ponderosa pines, horsetails, and sandhill cranes—the main actors of that afternoon. And I'd look for the life span of whatever radioactive contamination there might be at Los Alamos. Surely I could teach myself enough about the university library's science books and databases to find these simple, concrete numbers. I'd give it a couple of months, May and June, and then I might write a very short essay, maybe five or six pages, about that afternoon on the Pajarito Plateau.

Well, it didn't take me long to figure out that my questions were not so simple. Right away there was the matter of what exactly I meant by "this place." The canyon and plateau, yes, but what had been here before the Jemez volcano lay down the soil I'd walked on? And what did I mean by "here"? Certainly not the current latitude and longitude of northern New Mexico. So I started by defining "here" as the column of ground reaching straight down under my feet, my invisible link to the drifting continental plate. When my other actors appeared, where on the globe had "here" been, and what would it have looked like then?

While I was at it, I thought, I might as well start making the time line I'd been wanting for the past few years. Given my lifelong love of the natural world, my basic knowledge had some significant gaps: I'd left biology behind in ninth grade, and I'd never taken a geology course. (I'd made it through high school with chemistry, then satisfied my college science requirement with "physics for poets," a course nicknamed more for its lack of difficulty than for its imaginative potential.) Most of what I knew about the earth's ancient history was jumbled bits from recent and haphazard reading. I'd never been able to keep straight all those names for ages—Eocene, Carboniferous, Mesozoic—and I'd never before cared, but it quickly became clear that if I wanted my answers, I'd have to learn that vocabulary now. Anyway, I was coming to realize, I truly wanted to see how all the pieces fit together—continental drift, climate change, mountain building and inland seas, evolution. I wished to know more about what lay beneath the surfaces of the world.

My job was becoming huge. Still, I could begin.

When classes ended for the summer and my time was my own, I went to the university library, started typing into a computer . . . and promptly ran into trouble. Words I'd never seen and didn't know how to pronounce were suddenly everywhere: *ectomycorrhizae, Phanerozoic, cladistics.* I found almost nothing at the level of specialization I wanted. One major database showed only two entries under *horsetail,* one saying this is the primary food of breeding trumpeter swans, a happy fact, but not what I was looking for. In the library catalog, *Los Alamos Laboratory* produced a staggering 430 entries, most with incomprehensible or unsavory titles—"All secondary explosive hot-wire devices"; "Defect formation in 800-McV proton irradiated aluminum"—all stored in the terrifying microfiche government documents section.

One day I'd feel bewildered and frustrated; the next day stubborn and determined; every now and then intrigued, amused, or triumphant. I'd curse at the computer screen, sigh, stretch my sore neck and shoulders, laugh, groan, type some more. Variations of *pine* and *ponderosa* somehow turned up different lists every time I tried them. *Pine* produced nearly 2,000 entries, and *ponderosa pine* gave me 381, most of them as impenetrable as the *Los Alamos* titles. *Crane* provided some syllabic relief, as did *squirrel*, where I paused at *I Found a Baby Squirrel, What Do I Do?* and skipped over *My Mama's Dead Squirrel: Lesbian Essays on Southern Culture*, then hit gold at *The Natural History of Squirrels*. Like most of the promising titles, this one was checked out, so I learned how to recall it straight from the same computer screen.

Then there was the construction. In the midst of a massive and confusing expansion, the library changed its configuration daily. More than once I found myself juggling pack, pencil, sheaves of notepaper, and a slippery pile of heavy books up three flights of stairs that dead-ended at a locked door. I learned to begin each visit by picking up a fresh location guide and asking a librarian for directions.

While I was working, the science books migrated one call letter at a time from the fourth floor to the basement, where their new home was a dimly lit set of movable shelves. I'd start by peering at small signs until I found the aisle I wanted. Then I'd press a button. If someone was in one of the adjoining aisles, nothing would happen. Otherwise, some hidden motor would whir and the shelves would slowly part, allowing me to enter. At first I'd dart in, grab my book, and escape before the walls could close again and trap me. I made up bad metaphors—the shelves like continental plates, splitting and colliding in earthquakes and volcanoes—and I pictured my fossilized self, rediscovered at some far future time, compressed between evolution and chaos theory. With experience, though, I'd sit calmly on the floor and browse until someone asked me to move. A friend called this basement the most competitive space on campus, but I was learning to adapt and survive as I began to find pieces of answers to my questions.

And I do mean pieces. The date of a fossilized crane bone here, a revised date for the same fossil there—revised by several million years with no explanation that might help me judge my sources. In fact, competing dates were almost everywhere, so much so that I began to dismiss the usual variations of three or five million years as insignificant and became curious about the few dates that stayed constant. Patterns started to emerge— nothing I could call *objective*, but shapes that made sense to me. Wondering how scientists were deriving their dates, I kept running into my personal cast of characters: radioactive decay rates in organic carbons and in rocks, especially lava and compacted volcanic ash, sometimes focusing on uranium; ponderosa tree rings; the housekeeping methods of the pack rat, a cousin of the squirrel; the layers in ice cores; rock strata in cliff walls; the direction of magnetized minerals in lava. I found some of this information in numbers of years; some in era names like Upper Lower Devonian; some on maps and charts—a set of new languages I was slowly learning to interpret.

Occasionally I lit on a wonderful stray detail, material for my own private course in Biology and Geology for Poets, or maybe Science for Imaginers, the kinds of snippets that for me suggested whole worlds untethered by the rules of the familiar, where the ordinary was shot through with mystery. That the seismosaurus, apparently the largest land animal ever, had lived not far from Bandelier, this *earthshaker* twenty feet tall at the shoulder, more than a hundred feet long, the weight of a dozen large elephants. That our planet is an enormous magnet whose force field has reversed itself over and over, mostly once or twice every million years though seemingly at random, the north magnetic pole changing places with the south in response to some hidden motion in the molten rock of the outer core, far below the continental plates. Perhaps best of all, this luminous and enigmatic tidbit, a detail that took up residence in my imagination as though it owned the place: that except for a few egg-laying oddballs like the platypus and the echidna, all living mammals dream.

How on earth could I organize all these notes, these fragments of worlds? Maybe on pieces of paper taped to the hallway wall. I started at one end with the big bang and the formation of Earth—about one foot of wall for ten billion years, give or take a few billion. Then, with no regard to their relative duration, I assigned each major era its own fifteen or twenty inches and taped up a title sheet and a share of scribbled-on paper scraps. When I found new bits of data, I added slips of paper: large polar ice caps over the Sahara in the late Ordovician; iridium spike at the K-T Boundary sixty-five million years ago (good evidence at the New Mexico–Colorado border). I photocopied the best sketches of drifting continents and put them up, too.

I was totally caught up in this project, maybe even obsessive. Aided by a long series of cool, rainy days better passed indoors, I was spending most of my time immersed in my search, logging far more library hours than I'd done since graduate school nearly twenty years before. I just kept on reading—about fossil birds and plants, DNA and plate tectonics, the Puebloan cultures and nuclear waste. I skimmed the parts that seemed too specialized and kept looking for big patterns and resonant details. The hallway filled with notes that fluttered a little if I walked by in a hurry, though often I moved as slowly as I would in an art gallery, trying to absorb what I saw. When I'd read in a newspaper or magazine article that some bit of information I'd taken for definite was being revised, I didn't know whether to feel dismayed or excited, but I cut each new article out and added it to the wall. At some point during these weeks, I realized I'd read enough to know that I would never feel I'd read enough.

When the time seemed right, when I thought I had enough information to construct an outline, I bought a new set of colored markers and sat down with scissors and Scotch tape to transform the hallway scraps into a tidier booklet. I trimmed the maps into pretty shapes and outlined North America in green and the equator in red. I used all the colors of ink. I even sketched some pictures—a couple of weirdly shaped fossils from the Cambrian Burgess Shale, a giant dragonfly from the late Carboniferous, a Jurassic seismosaurus.

As I felt my way into all this new information, my questions sharpened, broadened, and got much harder. At what moment could it be said that an ancestor species had become a modern species? Exactly what makes a species itself, a crane a sandhill? To such enigmas, I came to realize, there could never be answers. And what level of classification did I care about? Ponderosas, pines, conifers, gymnosperms? The dates of these levels were vastly different. Slowly I started paying less attention to species and more to families, orders, classes.

The question of place grew more insistent and more elusive. Certainly that piece of ground in Bandelier where I'd rested and walked seemed less and less to have possessed anything that looked like a continuous identity. Seafloor, volcanic ash, more seawater, desert sands; a mountain range, another sea, more ash; all drifting around the globe, shifting attachments to vanished continents about whose histories we can only guess, Rodinia, Laurasia, Pangaea—with what kind of thread could landscapes like these be stitched to the eroding golden tuff of the present? But the hardest thing for me to grasp was the length of time. How could I even begin to imagine the emergence and disappearance of a whole mountain range? These matters grew fuzzier, more philosophical—so abstract, they seemed, so far beyond my human grasp. And yet I knew there was nothing more real, nothing, paradoxically, more urgent and intimate, than time and place and change.

And then came the flood. A rainy spring had turned into a rainy summer, twice as wet as usual. One weekend in late July it rained still more, until the soil on the foothills west of town was completely soaked and pools of water lay everywhere. On Monday night it rained again, in some places as much as ten inches in five hours—more than two-thirds the total for an average year in this semiarid place. A flash flood whipped through town. Tiny Spring Creek, normally a lazy, shallow 8 feet wide, burst into turbulence as much as 175 feet across and 16 feet deep. Five women drowned, hurled downstream by the power of the water; many others barely escaped, hauled by firemen in rafts from nearly submerged windows and toppling traffic lights; mobile homes piled up and splintered; a train washed off its track; bridges broke loose and floated.

In the basement of the closed library on campus, a few people were moving things out of the way of moisture seeping from the saturated soil through the walls. They didn't know that just outside to the west, where the new construction was complete and the landscapers had been building a sloping lawn, water was rising and pressing in. A window creaked, the concrete around it groaned, the workers ran through the maze of movable shelves for the stairs. The wall broke and water poured in, 8 feet deep. Every book was soaked, more than 460,000 volumes. Many were pulled from the shelves by the turbulence, their pages ripped loose into piles of indecipherable debris. Others, crammed tightly between closed aisles and swollen with water, bowed up on the shelves like stone arches.

On the foothills, trails and roads disappeared and tiny creeks exploded. Shrubby slopes cracked apart and slid, leaving raw new canyons 20 feet across. The skull of a bison emerged, dead maybe a thousand years, buried, perhaps, by another heavy rain. Time shifted into fast-forward. Local scientists called it a five-hundred-year flood, and in a few hours, in a small place, it did the geological work of centuries. In those hours, and in the chaos that followed, I caught a glimpse of the irregular pace of time and change.

With my ready source of reference books cut off, I turned to my paperback copy of Darwin's *On the Origin of Species*. I found myself reading and rereading his elaboration of a metaphor offered by the geologist Charles Lyell, a passage now oddly multiple and ironic, heavy with meanings: "I look at the natural geological record, as a history of the world imperfectly kept, and written in a changing dialect; of this history we possess the last volume alone, relating only to two or three countries. Of this volume, only here and there a short chapter has been preserved; and of each page, only here and there a few lines." I thought about the nature of what we know—what we think we have deciphered from books, from fossils, from rocks—how it is and always will be incomplete, how it all depends on so many other ways of knowing, so many layers of interpretation and imagination, all of them tentative, partial, changing.

I struggled to bring this all together into some kind of order, the flood, my research, my brightly colored time line, the feel of the Pajarito Plateau. I brooded about the way the earth emerges through volcanoes into itself, about the liquid nature of the world and everything in it, and I wondered about what happened to human values under the pressure of such thoughts. In what imperfect dialect might we speak of a woman's drowning and the twenty-four-thousand-year half-life of plutonium, a flooded library and the dreams of all mammals, the shape-changing earth and the voice of the crane in a winter sky?

*I*n these ways I pieced together a story about a place and a few of its inhabitants, a lacy strand of holes and guesses, a faint and broken whisper of what the earth itself might tell, if somehow layer by layer the ground beneath that trail in Frijoles Canyon might disappear, the past rise up to become the present, and time begin again.

For my hallway and booklet time lines, I hadn't worried much about proportions: one chunk of wall and one page each for the 13 billion years from the big bang to the Cambrian, the 70 million years of the Ordovician, the mass extinctions 65 million years ago, the 10,000 years of the Holocene. But now I needed a scale I could visualize, some analogy that was the right size for my human imagination, my human body.

So one day I sat down to work. I listed major dates with all their zeroes written out (4,550,000,000 years B.P., or before the present, for the formation of Earth; 400,000,000 for the appearance of horsetails; 360,000,000–290,000,000 for the Carboniferous), and then I started playing with a ruler and a calculator. I thought about miles and kilometers, yards and meters, feet and inches; I measured the length of my stride, the span of my hand, the middle joint on my little finger. I filled piece after piece of blank paper with numbers.

Finally I found a scale I could grasp, one I could use to tell my story.

Pick up a piece of ordinary typing or printer paper, and call it a century. Then hold a ream of this paper, a package of five hundred sheets, two inches thick, and in your hands you'll have 50,000 years. Now stand these packages side by side like books on a single very long library shelf, and picture yourself walking with me along that shelf towards today.

The story begins with the big bang, the first and most cosmic word, uttered somewhere between 10 and 18 billion years ago. If we call it 13.4, one number suggested by recent data from the Hubble space telescope, then our shelf will be just under eight and a half miles long. From this instant, the point from which we take our first step, comes every bit of matter and energy in the universe—in galaxies and nebulae, quasars and black holes, my body and yours, each gliding crane and burning star in the sky.

For close to six miles, we walk through a chaos of darkness and fire. Then, around 4.55 billion years ago, our solar system forms from the debris of vanished stars, and this planet collects itself into a swirl of radioactive elements, convection currents, magnetism, and gravity, then volcanoes, rain, an atmosphere. By the time we've walked another half mile, temperatures and air pressures have largely stabilized, and what we call life has probably begun. For the next two miles of shelf and more— another 3.3 billion years—bacteria dominate, as they will continue to do, in numbers and perhaps mass, as long as there's any life at all. In warm, shallow waters, cyanobacteria begin gathering into pillows that will harden into stromatolites, the oldest fossils known. The supercontinent Rodinia forms, then splits into pieces scattered around and below the equator, and the Canadian Shield, what will become the core of North America, is already intact. *Here,* beneath the Pajarito Plateau, the land changes and changes again, with erupting volcanoes and shallow seas, mountains thrust up and flattened, the climate cold, warm, cold again.

More than eight miles into our walk, not long after a major period of glaciation, in what will be called the Cambrian Event or Explosion, bacteria and other extremely primitive plankton, seaweeds, and soft-bodied creatures are joined by suddenly complex sea animals with hard body parts, shells and carapaces and rudimentary backbones. They make an astonishing array, their forms those of dreams and nightmares, the shapes a wildly imaginative child might invent—eyes at the ends of tubes, forked tails and crescent-moon helmets, fern-shaped feet, spikes and tentacles and claws and armored plates. One worm-like thing with seven pairs of spikes coming out one side and seven skinny tubes coming out the other will win the scientific name *Hallucigenia.* The first fish swim in fertile waters, and what will become the Sahara lies buried under ice near the South Pole. Then the first major extinctions occur, and evolution takes a leap sideways.

When the first land plants appear, it's 400 million years ago, a quarter mile away from today. Horsetails are among the earliest of them, and so by far the oldest of the small set of canyon dwellers that started me on this learning. By now, *here*—"this place"—floats somewhere near the equator, part of the northern continent Laurasia, sliding south towards the larger Gondwanaland, first just above and then beneath the warm, shallow seas. Fungi have begun their long and close involvement with land plants, and the earliest amphibians wander lazily across the sand.

A second great wave of extinctions occurs 40 million years later, marking the end of the Devonian and beginning of the Carboniferous. Horsetails, though, survive to flourish through the next 70 million years. They're as tall as trees, and they grow in great towering forests of tree-sized ferns, rushes, and club mosses. Tropical seas lie just to the south, home already to sharks and clams and gardens of crinoids, whose shadowy fossils suggest little octopus mops.

Just under two-tenths of a mile from the end of our imaginary bookshelf, around 300 million years ago, the continents begin colliding into the giant Pangaea. *Here,* just above the equator and inching now to the north, it grows more arid as the Ancestral Rockies start to rise. They will reach as high as ten thousand feet, maybe higher, and the ground far beneath the Pajarito Plateau is close to their watery edge. Somewhere dragonflies with two-foot wingspans hover over still pools. Spiders hunt their tiny prey, and large sail-backed reptiles forage for plants and meat. The first conifers, the phylum that will later come to include ponderosa pines, are beginning to grow uphill from the ferns and horsetails. Together they thrive through the completion of Pangaea. Then, around 245 million years ago, they survive the third great onslaught of extinctions, the largest ever, when more than half the known families of life disappear. This is the line we draw between the Paleozoic and the Mesozoic.

Over the next two hundred yards and 180 million years of

our shelf, Pangaea breaks apart very slowly, so slowly that for some 100 million years land animals still roam freely from one emerging continent to another. The Atlantic Ocean expands, the Ancestral Rockies erode, the Appalachians rise. Earth's surface convulses with volcanoes, and mysteriously, late in the Mesozoic era, its magnetic fields pause in their customary reversals. The planet grows warmer again, sea levels fall, then rise. Finally North America drifts alone to the northwest, huge seas cover its center, dividing it into two land masses, then recede, and some great force thrusts the second Rocky Mountains towards the sky.

Here, at the southern tip of this new range, the land during these eons is a mixture of floodplains, dunes, and volcanoes, a collection of rich habitats and ecotones. Tall conifers shade the last large amphibians and the first small mammals, sharks and dragonflies, all manner of dinosaurs, pterosaurs, and crocodilians. A fourth wave of extinctions makes way for the first birds; for forests thick with fan-leafed gingkos, palmlike cycads, and members of the pine family; and for the Jurassic supersaurus, ultrasaurus, and seismosaurus. One of these earthshakers will die and lie buried for 150 million years, until humans retrieve its fossilized remains. A single vertebra from its tail—a good cubic foot of bone, with another foot or more rising from its top like a giant handle—will lie in a glass case in the Museum of Natural History in Albuquerque, where I will study it, astounded.

The sea covers this land, then draws back. Flowering plants appear, forests of figs and eucalyptus, ebony and magnolias, palms and ivy, pine trees that look much like ponderosas. Just to the south, rain seeps through volcanic intrusions and ashfalls, picks up atoms of uranium, and deposits them in the buried remains of Jurassic conifers and horsetails.

Then, 65 million years ago, at what is called the K-T Boundary, a massive asteroid hits the planet with some five billion times the power of the bomb that destroyed Hiroshima. Almost all the large vertebrates vanish, along with 80 percent of the plants, most plankton, and many reef dwellers. (Since only lowland plants become fossils, there's no telling whether more upland plants survived.) Just seventy-two yards short of the end of our eight-and-a-half-mile shelf, this mass extinction, the fifth, creates the space for the next new world, the close of the Mesozoic and the beginning of the Cenozoic, the era of "new animals."

Enter the first cranelike birds, five and a half yards later and 60 million years ago, over what is, *here*, a tropical rainforest. Another eleven yards, and ponderosas are leaving clear fossils in a much cooler world. Five more yards brings a drier climate, open woodlands whose trees look like willows and cottonwoods, the bleaching bones of squirrels.

But such familiar traces of the present are misleading. In the museum in Albuquerque, murals of Cenozoic landscapes—all the way up to just 5 million years ago, a mere five and a half yards before today—are full of fantastic and largely unrecognizable mammals, mix-and-match collages of body parts: a rhino-tapir and a dog-mongoose; an armored lizard and a cow-sized pig; a fugue of teeth and tusks, antlers and horns, hides and fur; dozens of variations on the familiar themes of hippo, camel, and horse; elephant, deer, and lion.

Meanwhile, around 45 million years ago, a long series of massive volcanic explosions has begun in the southern Rockies, a series that will last nearly to the present. About thirty-five yards before today, the land under and around the Rocky Mountains begins to dome a mile upwards. New Mexico is covered with enormous volcanoes, some of them ten times larger than Mount St. Helens, and ash spews far and deep. The land cracks open from southern Colorado right through New Mexico. Slicing straight down into the mantle, thousands of feet deep, this Rio Grande Rift will widen towards the south to include the broad arid plain the Spanish will name the Jornada del Muerto. Finally I can pinpoint *where* I mean by *here*—on a continent just about in its present location, on the eroding shoulder of a large volcano on the western edge of the Rio Grande Rift.

When we're about ten yards from the end of our bookshelf, 9 or 10 million years ago, some cranes are recognizably sandhills. After another 6 million years, the early hominid *Australopithecus* has appeared, though not in the Western Hemisphere. Within our next two strides, the modern genera of tree squirrels develop, the Rio Grande becomes a single strand, the Rockies begin to erode into their current shapes, the genus *Homo* appears in Africa, an ice age begins, and finally, just 1.4 and 1.1 million years ago, the Jemez volcano, active already for some 13 million years, explodes. In two massive pyroclastic flows, avalanches of boiling debris and gases, it lays down the Bandelier tuff, the actual soil from which the Pajarito Plateau and Frijoles Canyon will emerge.

By the time humans arrive on this soil, some 10 or 11 thousand years ago, when summers are cool and wet, when ponderosas grow low and thick on the mountains and men use sharp points of volcanic obsidian to kill mastodons and dire wolves, camels and giant ground sloths, the canyon has eroded considerably, sometimes imperceptibly, more often in a flash. Finally we're at the end of our eight-and-a-half-mile walk, with only half an inch left on the shelf, a quarter of one ream of paper, little enough to hold in our hands without noticing its weight. When the Anasazi culture begins, we have just sixteen sheets, and by the time these ancestral Puebloan people carve their homes into these cliffs of tuff, a golden climb above the horsetail-edged creek, we're down to eight, six, four. Sometime during these centuries, some of these people begin to know themselves as members of the clan of cranes. With five sheets left, the oldest of the vanilla-scented ponderosas I'll pass along my wintery trail have sprouted.

On the final sheet of paper, that feathery slice of the present, my story of this place grows more precise and detailed, more immediate and personal. In 1916, Bandelier National Monument is established to protect the deserted cliff houses and kivas of Frijoles Canyon, about a year before my father's parents move to Albuquerque to treat my grandfather's tuberculosis. In 1939, Bosque del Apache National Wildlife Refuge first offers official shelter to wintering sandhill cranes, 150 miles south along the Rio Grande. In December of 1941, when Japan bombs Pearl Harbor, just seventeen cranes sleep among the cattails and bulrushes of the new refuge. In February 1943, a highly secret scientific laboratory opens on the Pajarito Plateau with the sole task of developing an atomic bomb. In June, my father is called to active duty in the Army Air Force. By the next summer, when small batches of plutonium, manufactured from uranium, have begun to arrive in New Mexico, he is in Oakland, working the midnight shift decrypting messages from the China-Burma-India theater.

Before dawn on July 16, 1945, the first atomic bomb is exploded at the Trinity Site—less than 30 miles east of Bosque del Apache, in the wide sweep of the Rio Grande Rift the Spanish had called the Jornada del Muerto. Most people translate this as the Journey of Death, but it might also have meant One Day's Journey into Death. On the distant Pajarito Plateau, a brilliant light illuminates the ponderosas and junipers. Four hours later—nine months and one day before my husband will be born—his parents are married, his father just home from the war in Europe and expecting to be sent to the Pacific. My father is already there, on the tiny island of Iwo Jima, an oasis of volcanoes and wreckage, an airfield and dead men buried.

At 4:52 A.M. on August 6, the B-29 bomber *Enola Gay* passes directly over the airfield at Iwo Jima on its way to decimate Hiroshima in a single flash of fire and lingering radioactivity. My father doesn't remember whether he was on duty, so I imagine him sleeping. Does the sound of the engines disturb his dreams, or has he by now slept through too many passing planes? On August 14, Emperor Hirohito announces over the radio the surrender of Japan, in what historian Richard Rhodes calls the "high, antique Voice of the Crane"—a Japanese phrase for the voice that commands complete attention. For the rest of the century, visitors will leave thousands and thousands of folded paper cranes at the memorial at Hiroshima, prayers for peace and healing.

On the Pajarito Plateau, the bomb-building escalates after the war ends. From 1945 to 1952, radioactive wastes are dumped untreated into Los Alamos Canyon. Uranium is mined from Jurassic soils across the West. In 1951, five months after the United States starts exploding nuclear bombs aboveground in Nevada—directed from Los Alamos National Laboratory—I am born. The Rio Grande Rift continues to widen, and small earthquakes shake its sides, around the laboratory and the cliff houses, south across the Jornada del Muerto and Bosque del Apache.

In 1952, the laboratory begins to bury its wastes, wrapped in plastic bags, corroding barrels, soggy cardboard boxes, most of it in long, shallow open pits carved like great misshapen kivas into the volcanic tuff of the Pajarito Plateau. The catalog of radioactive contaminants in this place makes a dark epic of threat, their names both familiar and strange, both tedious and insistent: numbered isotopes of americium, cesium, and cobalt; hafnium, iodine, plutonium; radium, sodium, and strontium; technetium, tritium, and yttrium; five kinds of uranium. Iodine lodges in thyroids; cesium in nervous systems; strontium, radium, and plutonium in bones.

They decay one invisible particle at a time, these rare and often beautiful metallic elements—*luminescent,* my dictionary says, *brilliant-white, silvery, silvery white*—shape-changing with tiny bursts of energy, always becoming something other than what they were. Some of their half-lives are short—6 hours, 3 days, 30 years. Others are longer, or much longer—430 years, 24,000 years (for man-made plutonium 239), 17 million years.

To think about the uranium isotopes, I want to slow down, hold the numbers up against my bookshelf time line, a mirror image now of the millennia yet to come. Less than a week for U-237; 159,000 and 245,000 years for U-233 and U-234. Twenty-three million years for U-126, roughly the time it has taken the Rio Grande Rift to open, widen, and fill with up to ten thousand feet of eroded debris. For U-235, the central element of nuclear chain reactions, 700 million years, far longer than there have been hard-bodied organisms on Earth. For U-238, the variety most abundant in those Jurassic sandstones, by the time just half the atoms buried at Los Alamos will have passed through their own kind of evolution, a chain of thirteen other radioactive incarnations ending finally in the stability of lead, it will be 4.5 billion years into the future. Four and one-half *billion* years: the nearly unimaginable age of our solar system, our sun and our Earth.

In piecing together my story about this place, this sunny, juniper-studded plateau and peaceful, shadowy canyon in northern New Mexico, I have not expected such an eerie and troubling full circle.

It reaches far beyond irony, this final twist of the numbers, nearly beyond language, maybe beyond our capacity to comprehend. Still, I keep trying. For some way to begin, I study early accounts of the Hiroshima and, especially, the Trinity explosions.

The mountains flashed into life, writes one woman who watched the Trinity blast from far-away Los Alamos. A Santa Fe reporter explains, "A small amount of matter . . . was made to release the energy of the universe locked up within the atom from the beginning of time." President Truman warns the Japanese to "expect a rain of ruin from the air, the like of which has never been seen on this earth." Trinity's official recorder mixes the Bible with the big bang, our culture's oldest creation story with its newest: "On that moment hung eternity. Time stood still. Space contracted to a pinpoint. It was as though the earth had opened and the skies split. One felt as though he had been privileged to witness the Birth of the World—to be present at the moment of Creation when the Lord said: Let there be light."

But it is not about birth, this business of atom bombs, not about beginnings. And so I think the best description belongs to Robert Oppenheimer, the director of the bomb-building project, who also turned to an ancient and sacred wisdom, the Bhagavad Gita. I have watched him on film, in grainy shades of gray; brushing something from high on his right cheek, he says: "Now I am become Death, the destroyer of worlds."

In January, John and I drove again to New Mexico, where we spent a strange few days exploring the Rio Grande from Bosque del Apache to Los Alamos, wandering between the landscapes of the crane and the landscapes of the bomb.

One afternoon we studied B-29 bombers, documentary film from World War II, and photos of nuclear explosions at Albuquerque's National Atomic Museum, then drove south until it was nearly dark. On a bridge over the Rio Grande, we stood shivering and straining to see while thousands of cranes moved over our heads making their unmistakable calls, their strong wings whooshing down the slope of the rift. Sometimes dark lines of shadow dropped from the sky and disappeared into the marsh along the banks.

In the morning we rose early and drove into the refuge at Bosque del Apache. Thick fog wrapped the ground. The sounds of birds came from every direction and none, clucks and rattles and whirs and splashes, amplified and dispersed by the moisture in the air. A clump of cranes would appear, their long necks and legs blurred by the fog, their palette of grays muted, then vanish again in a silent shifting of air. A bald eagle emerged from the mist, a hunched night heron, another dozen cranes, a fleet of snow geese, and always the sounds of life unseen.

That afternoon we wandered east across the Jornada del Muerto until we were as close as we could be to the radioactive soils of the Trinity Test Site. At dusk we watched the cranes gather again, then had a green-chili burger and a Tecate at the Owl Bar and Cafe, where workers from Los Alamos had stopped for refreshment as they prepared for the blast.

The next morning the sky was absolutely clear. At the refuge, we drove slowly along the loop road. Bald eagles waited on tall dead cottonwoods. The bare limbs of willows and saltcedars glowed russet. Birds were everywhere, floating and flapping, standing still like hieroglyphs perfectly doubled in the still water.

According to the Christmas bird count just a week before, more than thirty thousand ducks were here, and nearly nine thousand snow and Ross's geese, down from the twenty-four thousand on our first visit and the sixty thousand from a decade ago, but way up from the mere hundred that wintered here in 1950. Some twelve thousand sandhill cranes were in the refuge, with more along the river to the north and south. Their genus name, *Grus,* and their family name, Gruidae, share their root with *congruence*—they are the birds that come together, gathering in long threads over great distances and many eons. Around the world, most of their species and subspecies are in trouble, but the sandhills, at least for now, are increasing.

Once we stopped by a small ditch to watch a great blue heron. It held what looked like a young muskrat, its neck pinned firmly by the heron's beak, its skinny tail and four pink paws flailing wildly in the sunlight, each paw the shape and transparency of an infant's hand. Every now and then the bird would bend and dip into the water, then straighten and stand serenely while the muskrat flailed some more. Finally with a sudden lift of its beak, it swallowed and the muskrat disappeared into a lump sliding down the heron's long throat. If the muskrat cried out, we didn't hear it. The ditch water sent rippling waves of light across the heron's soft charcoal feathers, and the cranes beyond it continued their grazing.

We moved north to Santa Fe. We visited art museums and

the office of a citizen watchdog group, where I learned how to find out what wastes were buried at Los Alamos. We had lunch with the husband of my favorite cousin, Carol Ann, who just weeks before had fallen ill and died, stunning her family and plunging me into a river of terrible dreams.

In our motel room each evening, I lay on the floor with my head locked in a traction device that stretched my neck. Bone spurs and bulging disks were pressing on my spinal cord and pinching the nerves to my right arm, reminding me every few minutes how we're composed, stacks of vertebrae supporting long bundles of nerves, fine fibers stretched out along our limbs tying us into the world, its pain and its beauty. We move day by day encased in the illusion of autonomy, but really we're such vulnerable packages, so open in every way to the outside— flailing muskrats and serene deadly herons, cranes and bomb-builders, even the giant vanished seismosaurus—all of us members of the phylum Chordata, the clan of backbones, all of us kin. I thought about the vertebrae of the sandhills, how they protect the long, coiled tracheas that create those extraordinary harmonies, that commanding, haunting, ancient voice of the crane. I mourned for my cousin, whom I loved. And I pondered something I'd heard the Dalai Lama say a few months before, that as he grew older he wanted to spend more time in meditation, alone like a wounded animal.

Finally we drove up to Los Alamos, to the local history museum and the science museum. We watched more old films, studied wartime documents that had been declassified only in the 1970s and '80s, and read signs about radioactive isotopes, underground bomb testing, the new problem of safeguarding weapons-grade plutonium. Then we found the lab's public reading room, where I spent a couple of hours trying to decipher technical documents about waste disposal and making a list of radioactive isotopes buried in the soils of the Pajarito Plateau.

I was almost finished with my research. When I got home, I'd find the half-lives to complete my list, and then I'd stop working on this project, at least for now. I'd learned a lot since that sunny winter afternoon when the cranes passed overhead as I lay dreaming on the side of an old volcano. I had answers for many of my specific questions, though none of them had turned out to be simple or permanent. For the larger questions, it seemed clear, complexity and uncertainty would be the only constants, any conclusion I might draw always temporary, particular to a single set of circumstances, a single scale of proportion. There was no way to fix the essence of a place or a time, a species or even a pattern of change. There was no way to see the world simultaneously as a shape-shifting swirl of rock and water, gravity and magnetism, as a living kaleidoscope of creation and extinction, and as my own vivid and present home, the single moment of my own life. At most, I might hope for an occasional, fleeting, indecipherable instant of vision, of intuition, and even this, I thought, I could not trust.

When the day was nearly over, we drove into Frijoles Canyon for a last glance. I had one more simple question. I couldn't remember how I had known on that earlier winter visit that horsetails grew along the sides of the creek, how that detail had made it past the snow and ice and winter-dead foliage into my tiny pocket notebook. I jumped out of the car and walked quickly up the trail beneath the crumbling cups of cliff houses, glowing again in the last of the afternoon light. No horsetails on this bank, where the sun had melted most of the snow. I crossed a small bridge and started more slowly back down the shady side of the canyon, crunching carefully through the icy crust, peering through the dusk at the broken sticks in the snow around me. Still no horsetails. John had joined me by now, helping me search, and the silence said we were alone in the canyon.

At last, there they were. Still green, still pliable, finger-thick stalks of that most ancient land plant, a miniature forest of horsetails thrusting up through the snow into the dim and chilly light. As I ran my cold fingers over their smooth surfaces and rough dark joints, I thought once more about how much was happening here in this still place, whether I could see it or not. Coyotes slept while ravens floated on the day's last warmth, radioactive elements threw out their invisible poisons, the ponderosas gathered sustenance from the hidden webs of fungus that wrapped their roots, and beneath a blanket of fallen needles, their seeds prepared to sprout.

Under my feet the ground dissolved, as it always has and always will. The moon shone above the cliffs, and a great horned owl called mournfully as we walked together down the darkening trail.

II

The Edge of Winter

---

*T*he following spring was exceptionally brilliant. Pasque flowers and sand lilies splashed across the foothills, and wild plums, chokecherries, and shooting stars lit each tiny creek. At our house, every bloom ignited another—daffodils, flamy tulips, violets, crabapple and apricot trees, lilacs, iris, peonies. Even the birds seemed early and exuberant, a meadowlark loud in February, white pelicans skating across the April sky. In May, at dinnertime, we sat at our picnic table and listened while courting nighthawks roared and snipe called like moving water.

I spent many hours outside. I took my work to the yard, piled books and papers in my lap, set my binoculars near to hand. Marmot and Weasel sniffed and barked and ran madly about, then came back to lie pressed against my legs in the sun. I had every reason to feel happy.

And sometimes I did. But much more often I felt trapped somewhere between the blues and outright depression, as if I were encased in some kind of protective suit and helmet that didn't work right, letting in all the world's toxins but cutting me off from everything heartening. Sitting in my yard, I'd think, "What a pretty song that meadowlark has," then a moment later I'd be brooding about declining songbird numbers and habitat loss. I'd glance at the newspaper, merely glance, and another murder would jump out at me, another rape, fatal car crash, flesh-eating disease. I'd flip on the TV or radio hoping for a weather forecast and hear the screams of children fleeing a massacre in Kosovo or men in dark suits worrying about forest fires covering central Mexico.

I remembered my mother's advice to a moody, anxious teenage daughter—and maybe, I thought now, to herself as well: *Count your blessings.* Yes, they are many, I'd think, and yes, I'm grateful. Then I'd start sliding. Of course I don't deserve my good fortune. It could vanish any time, and even if it doesn't, how could I forget about all the people who haven't had my luck, all the animals, plants, whole landscapes? Everywhere I looked I saw devastation—our violence against ourselves, and worse, the planet-sized wave of extinctions we are setting in motion. Against such pain and loss, my little doings were profoundly trivial, and any comfort I could take in my personal list of blessings smacked of selfishness and bad faith.

I felt beaten down, and not just in my mind. I'd had walking pneumonia twice that year and was on my way to an asthma diagnosis—too much dirty air for too long. The bulging disks, arthritic bone spurs, and pinched nerves in my neck still hurt, sometimes just a little, sometimes a lot, adding up to low-grade but chronic pain. As an insult added to injury, I needed bifocals, too. I'd been carrying a prescription around in my wallet for nearly a year, and though I didn't want to admit it, the time had clearly come to face up: I could barely read in the evenings when my eyes were tired, and my glasses were covered with a gauze of scratches, perhaps in itself part of the reason I felt wrapped in a personal cloud. The slow decay of the physical: I'd been pondering it for a year and more. Now I was experiencing it in my own tissues and bones.

Were my blues only this, that I was getting older and not liking it? Was I caught in the unthinkable cliché of a midlife crisis? Or was my life out of balance, my body chemistry, my psyche, in some way I should be able to fix with therapy or medicine? Perhaps so, I thought, yet none of these explanations felt adequate; this mood wasn't just about *me*. I felt more as if my mental immune system had shut down, leaving me unable to resist all the bad news. After all, I was tied into the world around me, flesh and mind and heart, not separate from it. My body was simply part of the world's body. Why wouldn't I feel at least some of what was wrong with the planet?

Still, this was hardly a productive way to spend my life. I was getting impatient with myself, sick of my own despair. I had to do something to make myself feel better.

Right, I said to myself. *Do something.*

So I started with light. Years before I'd noticed that my spirits drooped in the fall. As the days shortened, I'd grow lethargic; I'd feel trapped in routine; my vision of a future would narrow and pale. I'd read just enough about seasonal affective disorder (with its pat acronym, SAD) to recognize my symptoms with some relief. SAD, it seemed, might account for how hard I'd found living in Ohio's cloud belt. It might mean my frequent autumn blues didn't reflect some profound laziness. It could also have something to do with my love of high places where the light is especially intense. SAD couldn't be my problem in this brilliant spring, but still I might do a little research about it.

I called my friend Gerry, an immunologist who knows about things like this, and got some tips to help me begin. Then I went to the library for my first significant visit since last summer's flood. It was still a mess there, the expansion project delayed by newly urgent repairs, the basement darkened, bookless, and barricaded. On the computer catalog, book after book bore the label FLOOD. Now on the third floor, the science section looked downright pitiful, just a few books lying askew on each gray shelf, the ones that someone had had checked out last July. (Donated replacements would trickle in over the next couple of years, and restored volumes would return even more slowly.) But with a librarian's help, I made my way with reasonable dispatch to undamaged parts of the library: medical encyclopedias, electronic sources, and recent journals.

In a few minutes I had my search words—not just *seasonal affective disorder,* which pointed me to a wealth of psychological and sociological research focused especially on people living where winters are darkest, but also the biological terms I was more interested in: *chronobiology, circadian clock, photoreceptors.* It seemed I'd stumbled on a hot topic.

An hour or two later, I had deciphered a general sense of the mechanism: Light hits our photoreceptors, which are mostly in the rods and cones of our eyes. Then, perhaps carried by blood, it moves to a region in our brains called the suprachiasmatic nucleus. (What could "light" possibly look like in blood? What kind of thing had "it" become by now? And what was a suprachiasmatic nucleus? Was it big or tiny, hard or soft? I shrugged these questions aside and plowed on.) Next "it" interacts with something in another brain region, the hypothalamus. There it produces or alters some hormones. In the form of these hormones, light finally acts on our sleep patterns, moods, mental health, maybe even our immune systems and physical health. Aiming to boost this process, the most common treatment for SAD is extra light aimed usually at the eyes . . . but not always. According to one intriguing study, photo-therapy might also be aimed at the backs of the knees. We have photoreceptors there, too, these researchers suggested, and likely elsewhere, maybe many more places, under our skin.

I was already spending a lot of time outdoors. Still, I certainly *felt* that I needed more light, and surely it couldn't hurt to increase my dosage a little. I started taking off my sunglasses now and then. Without those vision-sharpening prescription lenses, the world would blur, and in the sudden painful brightness I'd have to concentrate not to squint, to hold my eyes wide open. One day I tried lying in my yard with the backs of my knees bare to the sky. I felt silly doing it, of course, and uncomfortable, too—the ground was hard and bumpy in patterns I didn't match, the grass pricked my skin, and wandering ants kept tickling me. But it did cheer me up, though perhaps not so much through my suprachiasmatic nucleus and hypothalamus as through Marmot and Weasel, who read my posture as an invitation to scramble onto my back and lick my neck and ears. Stop thinking about UV damage, pollution, ozone layers, I told myself. You can't fix them right now. Just do this: Feel how permeable you are to light, to air, to other living things. Feel the ground, the ants, the dogs. Feel how concretely you're woven into the fabric of the world.

As I lay in the sun, I thought, too, of what I'd learned about the Pajarito Plateau, the story I'd put together of that world's old body, and I began to wonder whether my new knowledge was contributing to my sadness. Such a tale of catastrophes, floods and explosions, mass extinctions—surely the message was that transience was and always had been everything. I'd been contemplating the problem of scale, how to reconcile the long rhythms of geology and evolution with the shorter ones of everyday life, the shifting of continental plates with the minute grindings of my neck vertebrae, the cosmic with the immediate. It had been a matter of curiosity, at first, an intellectual question. But things had changed. The lesson I wanted to be a comfort—that no matter what caused it, each destruction made way in the long run for something new—now felt like a wound. What I'd come to understand as vast and inescapable paradoxes had somehow condensed into an emotional shadow, and disaster had revealed itself as the stuff of each passing ordinary day. What truly mattered, every tiny particular of our days, or nothing at all but the slow unfolding of the universe? Deep time spoke of the latter. How then should I live my life?

Maybe, in short, I'd focused my vision too much on the matter of loss. If I chose a more heartening subject, could I cheer myself up with more research? And so I decided upon my summer's agenda: I would learn more about the alpine tundra near my home, work at seeing a familiar and beloved place with new eyes. I'd get out of the library and into the field, outside and high in bright sun, clear dry air, scouring wind, in a place that had always lifted my heart and filled me with exhilaration and life. Instead of focusing on deep time and extinction, I'd pay attention now to toughness and adaptation, to all the intricate ways life finds to make it through the dark times, the cold of winter.

I'd give myself a lesson in survival.

June seventh, Trail Ridge Road, Rocky Mountain National Park, just before noon. Ptarmigan Day.

I had offered to drive because I love this road, have loved it my whole life, how it swoops and twists and climbs so high so quickly that driving feels like flying, flying through rising layers of worlds, a new one every few miles: low meadows purple with wild iris, grassy stands of ponderosas, dense woods of Douglas fir, lodgepole pine, new-leafed aspen, two miles above sea level, snow still deep along the roadside, bands of slender Englemann spruce and subalpine fir alternating with broad, brush-fingered limber pines, each layer a world of more light, stronger winds, sharper cold, deeper winter, then just below treeline, Rainbow Curve, a spot wide enough for a score of cars to pull off . . . and all at once the day was turning into a small adventure.

It was a traffic jam—and also clearly something of a party. Some hundred SUVs and pickups sat scattered every which way, even a few sedans like mine, mostly local folks, to judge from the license plates. Children dashed about and tightroped along the low stone wall dividing the small parking area from the long, steep drop-off to the north. Adults wandered around with cameras and sandwiches in hand, chatted with each other, admired the view, and waited. Even now, a week into June, winter wasn't over. The road had opened for the season only two weeks ago (with a bigger, more official party John and I had found ourselves joining); snow had fallen yesterday, as it would keep doing nearly every day for a while longer; and Trail Ridge was closed again from here on up until the plows could finish their job.

Closed, that is, to everyone else. I was following the man with the key: Ken Giesen, a Colorado Division of Wildlife biologist who was teaching today's class about white-tailed ptarmigan. We'd spent the morning at park headquarters looking at slides, and now, in a caravan of two, we were inching through the crowd while my passengers joked through open windows with the folks we were leaving behind. Finally we reached the gate. Ken unlocked it, locked it behind us, and we were heading into the sky.

From here, it didn't take long to get through the last of the forest. We passed the site of an old fire, where a few trunks stood white, stark, and solitary more than a century after they burned. As a child I'd been impressed by these remnants, which my father said had looked about the same when he first came in the 1930s, and I marveled yet again at this sign of the harsh climate, how it slows new growth nearly to nothing. Beyond the burn, the trees grew fewer, shrank and twisted and became more picturesque, until each one might have belonged on a postcard. Finally the forest withdrew into tiny low islands of survivors, cushions a few yards across and just hip high. This was krummholz, a good word to pronounce; in German, it means crooked wood. Here one tree might be three feet tall, ten feet across, and many hundred years old. They're strong enough to stand on, a fact I once tested somewhere else, and if you have to, you can work your way under them to hide from hail or lightning, which I have also done, though their comfort will be tenuous.

Leaving these trees behind makes some people uncomfortably exposed, I knew, but it always exhilarates me. As I drove through the krummholz and out into the tundra, I felt as if I were crossing over an edge, away from any ordinary protection and into some radical and cleansing kind of openness.

From here on for nearly ten miles, the road would stay above the trees, a sinuous thread across the gently rolling uplands that top this part of the Front Range of the Rockies. We were retracing an ancient migratory and hunting route between the Great Plains and the green valleys to the west, one used by elk, deer, bighorn sheep, and people, most recently Ute and Arapaho women and children, then tourists, hikers, ptarmigan searchers. Not far past Rainbow Curve, I'd heard, if you walked uphill and looked very carefully, you could find the remains of a game-drive system several thousand years old, where hunters once funneled animals into a narrow space and then ambushed them—three long lines of rocks that don't quite match their surroundings and a scattered handful of stone hunting blinds; later this summer, I resolved, I'd try to find this site for myself.

These uplands are high enough that all through the last glaciation they remained above the ice, though just barely, and so everywhere to the sides the land drops sharply off into glacier-cut cirques and valleys. After its sometimes edgy route to the top, mostly the road rests safely in the middle of broad meadows, a drive even a flatlander at the helm of an RV can enjoy. But where the heads of glaciers once drew near to each other, the road runs right against cliff tops and meadows vertical enough that a straying vehicle would plummet a couple thousand feet, and many visitors hug the inside doors of their cars, ready to leap. The next named bit of the road after Rainbow Curve is Knife-Edge, where I've sometimes looked almost straight down on bighorn sheep or elk grazing just a few yards away. I used to be terrified of falling in places like this, too, my imagination full of potential disasters. But once I was old enough to drive with confidence, my fear vanished.

Driving here demands attention in any case, but I'm used to it, in fact I enjoy it, especially when I have the road to myself—though just as I thought this, Ken's brake lights flashed on, he slowed sharply, I slammed on my brakes, and two giant snowplows appeared from behind a pile of rocks and roared past us.

It was an adrenaline moment. Their drivers must have been surprised to see us, too, but they didn't show it as we exchanged the westerner's greeting for empty roads, a laconic hand raised from the steering wheel, really just the index finger, maybe a slight nod, enough to say, *Howdy, nice day.* I was too busy remembering to breathe to register whether these were ordinary plows or the much scarier ones they use to carve the road out in the spring, chained tires up to my shoulders and two long fangs framing a pair of blades, each an enormous spiral of sharp metal lying on its side. Just here the wall of snow was maybe ten feet tall, and I was driving through a tunnel of white and blue.

A few seconds later, the walls were gone and the ground was mostly bare of snow, just low patches strewn about in a pattern you might make with a wide but almost empty paintbrush over a rough surface. It's not the snow that makes this a hard place to live, in fact, but the wind. The wind moves the snow around all winter into drifts, shallows, and dry spots, matching the contours of the land so precisely that every year the same pattern is repeated, and so quite different plant communities mark the varieties of snow cover, each one adapted to fit a very particular set of living circumstances. The deepest drifts melt so late that some summers they never disappear, small reminders of how glaciers begin. Other patches of land stay mostly bare, unprotected from the cold, the sharp and desiccating ground blizzards, and the burning sun. Winter winds often top 100 miles an hour, sometimes 120. When I asked once at headquarters if there was a weather station above timberline along Trail Ridge, the ranger hesitated for a moment, then said, "I don't think so, now. There used to be one, but the anemometer kept blowing away."

And no wonder, I thought, as my heart slowed again and I dropped farther back so I could feel free to look out over the curve of tundra and into space. There's nothing to stop the wind, just miles of valleys and mountains to churn it up, channel it, send it swirling and scouring in broad vigorous gales over the high spots and down again. We were about twelve thousand feet above sea level now, and though higher peaks rose in the distance, even a few gentle hills just by the road, still, from the long line of this ridge, the world looked as if it were under one of those convex lenses that turns everything into a dome—with me at the center top and the whole landscape dropping away from me.

Just past the Alpine Visitor Center, Ken pulled over to park where the road hairpins to the south, at the spot the maps call Medicine Bow Curve. I think of it as Poetry Curve, myself, for all the places with good names you can see from here: the Medicine Bow Mountains, the Snowy and Mummy Ranges, the Rawahs, the headwaters of the Cache La Poudre River and the Colorado. And just to the west are the Never Summer Mountains. As a child growing up in Denver, I'd always waited eagerly for my first glimpse of this range, hidden from my home by intervening peaks, visible only when we'd reached the highest point on this pass. I'd been eager for the view itself, a spectacular jagged ridge of white, but also for my chance to savor the name, the best one of all, the way it enticed me to imagine a land of endless winter, of remoteness, cold, and snow. It pleased me today that our search for the elusive and iconic ptarmigan was beginning just here.

A few minutes later, out of the car and newly wrapped in several layers of warm clothes, sandwich in my pocket, I was diving over the high pile of plowed snow at the road's edge.

The trail was more than half white, the deeper snow at that stage of invisible melting where with every step I took my boot was equally apt to stay on top of the crust, slide out from under me, or sink through to the ground. The sky was a hybrid, too, mixing blue with clouds likely to bring more snow, and while the sun felt warm, the breeze was chill. I was toasty from the car, my feet almost hot under their heavy boots and thick socks, but I knew this comfort wouldn't last.

Ken carried a small tape recorder in one hand, an odd-looking fishing pole in the other. Since he'd been banding white-tailed ptarmigan up here for many years, he knew just where they'd be getting ready to nest and seemed confident we could find one today. But I couldn't quite believe it.

It wasn't that I'd never seen these birds. Long ago, when I was a teenager in love with mountain climbing, in a high cirque cupping a tarn so clear that it seemed lifeless, I'd come across a pair whose feathers so matched the lichen-covered rocks and alpine flowers of high summer that I could barely find them even after I knew just where they were, no more than ten feet from me. I hadn't even known such a bird existed, and I was mesmerized by how they materialized out of the tundra. One winter much later, I had seen a large flock of them, their white feathers showing against white snow only because they cast shadows in the bright sun. And a few Octobers past, not far from here in the national park, John and I had spent a long time watching a small flock whose feathers had half changed to winter white, nearly invisible, again, at the edge of a snow patch. They didn't seem to mind our presence, and I lay on the chilly ground and inched closer until they were just a long arm's reach away and I could hear their soft clucking.

All three of these encounters had been accidental, even startling. More than that, really. For me these birds had become emblems—of high mountains, of the perfect matching of creature to place, a self to its world, and of the potential everywhere for a moment of pure surprise, the sudden appearance of what had been hidden but was always there. And this morning's class—the science, charts, numbers, maps, details—all this had only honed the mystery, given me a glimpse of what this bird knows, such intricate ways to survive hard winters, in fact to thrive in them. I could hardly believe that we could park our cars, walk a bit, and find one to catch, just like that.

Ken stopped and switched on his tape recorder. Static in the background, a welcoming tumble of low-pitched chatters or chuckles. Then, in a switch of tone so sudden it made me jump, two or three short, ear-piercing screams—the sound of a male ptarmigan announcing his presence.

"This time of year," Ken had told us earlier, "if you play the tape early or late in the day, often a bird will fly right at you." I struggled to quiet my breathing—the air here is noticeably thinner than where I live, nearly seven thousand feet downhill, and even on a level trail the snow made walking harder. I listened. Nothing. "There!" he said, and pointed. "Hear it? Down there." He played the tape again, waited half a minute, then plunged off the trail.

I hadn't heard a thing except Ken, his tape, the wind in my ears, my own lungs and heart. But I took the leap of faith and followed.

Damn. The steep slope and snow cover made my every step a gamble, no guessing what lay underfoot, rock pile, hollow, or tussock. Worse, right away my knee started to hurt. I'd spent much of the past two weeks hiking as high as I could get in the melting snow, jumping over the ubiquitous rivulets, sinking thigh deep in soft drifts. I hadn't thought I was overdoing it, but clearly I'd been wrong, and one knee had ached more each day. Though I'd seen the doctor and started on some anti-inflammatory drugs, it was too soon for a cure.

As I slowed and finally stopped, Ken leapt away down the hillside like an elk or a bighorn sheep, making it look simple. I'll wait here, I thought. Most of my classmates hadn't even stepped off the trail, and if Ken caught the bird, he'd bring it back up to show us. I looked for someplace to perch. Snowy ground, snowy knee-high tangles of willow, snowy slabs of rock: there, that book-sized chip of ice-skimmed granite, that would do.

The truth was, I didn't really mind stopping at all. I love to do this, just sit still somewhere in the mountains with nothing on my agenda and nobody to talk to. For these moments I generally don't think about anything in particular, certainly not about myself. Maybe I remember past visits and daydream about others that might come. Words might pass through my mind, *willow, Never Summer, granite, raven.* I lose my sense of passing time. When it's windy, I imagine I can feel clear air blowing between the cells of my brain, sweeping out the spaces the way a winter chinook will rid our yard of dead leaves. In a place where the view is wide—as it is on a mountaintop, along a ridgeline, on this hillside—I might contemplate the nature of exposure, what it means to be truly *out there* in the world, un-protected, open to whatever might happen. Most of all, I simply take in the view. I wait to see what might happen, what might reveal itself, where my attention might settle, what I might recognize for the first time, or again.

The history of this place, I'd learned in the past few weeks, was much like the one I'd traced the summer before for the Pajarito Plateau: sea bottoms becoming mountaintops, erosion, faulting, folding, continents running into each other, volcanoes. The dinosaurs disappeared, a new mountain range emerged, and newer layers weathered off as the land rose, until what remained on the surface—what I had driven through today, what I was sitting on now, I was pleased to know—was very ancient, Precambrian granitic and metamorphic rock ranging from 900 million to 2.5 billion years old. About 2 million years ago, the Pleistocene Ice Age began, a series of advances and retreats of ice sheets and glaciers, with the most recent glaciation reaching its peak 18 or 20 thousand years ago, less than an inch away from the present on my reams-of-paper, deep-time bookshelf, yet long enough ago that the landscape would have seemed wildly un-familiar.

On a day like this, with plenty of snow around, it wasn't so hard to imagine what it might have looked like when blue rivers of ice still filled most of the space below me—like a vast sea of cloud, land rising like islands out of mist. The skies would have been grayer and wetter than today's, and the snow would have swirled before even wilder winds, freezing hurricanes like those that carve their way to this day over the enormous ice sheets of Antarctica and Greenland. Though I'd been up here nearly every summer of my life, it had been years since I'd come this early in the season, and everything looked colder, harsher, and more dramatic than I'd expected.

What a view! Complex layers of white and deepening blue shadows stretched into the far distance, cut laser sharp by the intense light and attenuated atmosphere. I felt wholly alone on the mountainside, all bundled up and braced against the wind, nothing between me and the sun, cold ground under my body, cold air on my face and in my lungs, eyes wide open, just watching and waiting, waiting.

The ground, where I could see it, was matted flat and brown. Nothing moved, it seemed, but the air, no creature breathed but me. Yet I knew that life must be everywhere around me. But where? In what bodily forms? How did they do it, the inhabitants of this alpine tundra? Exactly how did they manage the dark times, the long, cold winters? Where did they find the energy—and the courage—for their annual explosions of creation and what looks like joy?

On that day—Ptarmigan Day, as I would come to call it—I didn't yet have many concrete answers for these questions. Although for most of my life I had felt at home here, both on Trail Ridge in particular and more generally in Colorado's alpine tundra, I'd never really studied the ecology of this landscape. But in the following months I learned much more, enough to draw for myself a cluster of Trail Ridge portraits, portraits that surprised me again and again in their details. It wasn't just what they implied about the difficulty of the environment, though these lessons were clear. What I found most bracing was what the details showed me about the many creative ways life finds to adapt.

Winter underlies everything about this place. Typically, summer lasts just forty days between frosts, and snow may fall any day of the year. Coloradans joke that our high country has two seasons, winter and July, and at least twice I've been in road-closing squalls on Trail Ridge on Independence Day. Even for short walks on summer days I carry earmuffs against sudden cold winds. By late August, snowstorms grow more frequent and temperatures drop. Soon the snowplows are back to regular work, and if in September John and I want to drive or hike up here, we call first to ask whether the road is open for the day. Sometime in October, the Park Service locks the gates and abandons the tundra to the snow and the winds.

Nearly half the winter days, gusts reach hurricane force over the most exposed spots. On nearby peaks, they may blow at more than 170 miles an hour. I have tried to ski up the closed road to see and feel this for myself, but I've never gotten far. Even in the forest, the icy wind cut right through my warmest clothes and blinded me with tears, and so much snow had blown off the pavement I had to take my skis off and put them back on whenever the trees thinned or thickened. For scientists monitoring studies above the trees, conditions are much worse; they have to struggle to find their way, even to stay on their feet, and so there's relatively little information on winter up here.

Ground blizzards erase vision and mark every bump and curve on the land with drifts. While beneath these drifts it's remarkably calm, moist, and warm, as much as sixty degrees warmer, in the wind-scoured areas, the ground freezes ten or fifteen feet deep long before the heavy insulating snows come in April and May.

No wonder it looked so dead around me just a week into June. Yet summer was just hours away, as I realized when I returned five days after Ptarmigan Day to explore some more, this time on my own. I walked out over the tundra until I found a rock big enough to shelter me from the wind, and then I lay flat against the ground, now quite a bit less snowy, traded my sunglasses for a magnifying glass, and found a much different landscape. In a space the size of my hand was all of this: a tiny patch of bare soil; one bit of quartz crystal, one of white granite bright with mica and four colors of lichen; a loose fragment of another lichen, sage green and branched; some decaying elk droppings and part of a dead plant that looked like the inside of a glass millefleur paperweight, dense with dried rosettes; some fine blades of grass; two narrow-leafed plants; something ferny and succulent; a stonecroplike plant so minuscule that a dime would cover fifteen complete stalks and their leaves; a fatter relative tinged with purple; and a cluster of alpine forget-me-nots.

And this miniature world was just what I could see with my own nearsighted eyes and a two-dollar magnifying glass. What I really needed was a set of interchangeable or, better still, combinable lenses, a wardrobe of vision expanders: microscope eyes to see the very tiny; X-ray eyes like Superman's to see beneath the ground; Geiger-counter eyes to check for radioactivity; time-lapse eyes for the very slow; wide-angle eyes for whatever just happened at the moment to be somewhere else nearby; maybe time-travel eyes for the past and the future. With tools like these, what else in the wintery landscape surrounding me could I have seen?

Of course I would have seen the lichens. They are among the tundra's most conspicuous and abundant inhabitants. Yet they lead lives full of paradoxes largely hidden from ordinary vision. And, I was surprised to find, these paradoxes also spoke directly to my own recent preoccupations. Again and again, these modest little organisms would turn out to be intimately tied into issues much larger than I could have expected.

Clearly lichens know how to survive. Like horsetails, they're among the oldest forms of life on land; the earliest undisputed fossil is some four hundred million years old. Oddly, though, DNA studies indicate that today's varieties have not descended from these early forms. Instead, the "lichen lifestyle" (as even lichenologists call it) has developed several times, independently.

A lichen is actually a community of organisms so tightly

interwoven that they act as one. Strands of fungus wrap and protect algal cells, usually ordinary green algae, sometimes cyanobacteria or blue-green algae, the kingdom of organisms that built those earliest fossils, the stromatolites. The fungus provides structure and protection; the photosynthesizing algae provide food. Some biologists call this relationship "controlled parasitism," in which the fungi get the better part of the deal. But ecologists regard it as a highly successful symbiosis, a co-operative arrangement good for both partners, one that allows them to grow and thrive under otherwise impossible circum-stances. As one fungi specialist put it, "The components of a lichen can consequently perhaps be viewed as two organisms united in adversity."

In the form of more than fifteen thousand species, lichens manage to live in a staggering range of habitats: not just these high mountain ridges and peaks, but rainforests too, the Arctic and Antarctic, hot and cold deserts. Though they're poor com-petitors, they can live where other plants can't. And they're per-sistent. A few alpine species may survive more than a thousand years, perhaps as much as forty-five hundred years.

Nearly always, maybe always, they reproduce asexually, re-leasing very small particles that include bits of both fungus and alga. Or fragments of an established lichen will break off and start a new life somewhere else. They grow very slowly, nor-mally just millimeters per year. One species common in alpine places, *Rhizocarpon geographicam*, or map lichen, grows so slowly, only about half a millimeter a year, that sometimes, crossing chasms of scale, geologists use it to date the retreat of glaciers—or, one might say, to map the geography of the past.

But lichens also keep a sharp lookout for opportunity, when they can act with remarkable speed. In bad conditions, their metabolisms shut down and they take in almost no nourishment. Then when water appears, if there's enough light, they can start photosynthesizing within minutes, making food from sunlight, sometimes even at temperatures a little below freezing. I have created this transformation myself—poured water over a patch of dry lichen on a sunny day, then watched as brittle turned pliant, brown became green, and what seemed dead revealed itself to be alive.

This resurrection can happen largely because (unlike flowering plants) lichens have no waxy outer cuticle. By letting them respond quickly to small amounts of light and water, and thus to thrive in harsh environments, their thin skin has provided over the long run an enormous adaptive advantage. More recently, though, it has also put them at risk by leaving them vulnerable to damaging air pollutants, especially sulphur dioxide, a major part of ordinary smog. Dirty air will kill most lichen species; clean air allows them to recolonize deserted spaces; and so lichen monitoring has become a useful tool for tracking air quality.

Lichens also absorb ionizing radiation. In this case, they do so without damage to themselves, perhaps partly because radiation wreaks its havoc on the genetic level, where for these organisms things happen extremely slowly. They're relatively immune both to the ultraviolet rays that can cause skin cancer and to whatever radionuclides we put into the atmosphere through nuclear explosions and accidents. Indeed they can absorb enormous amounts of radioactivity; in one experiment, they survived a dose of one thousand rads a day for almost two years, continuing to grow while all the nearby vascular plants died. Less than one day of this treatment would kill a person.

Scientists started keeping careful watch over radionuclide

concentrations in lichens during the years of aboveground nuclear testing, when global fallout levels were high. When I searched in one large lichen database for *radionuclides*, I found that much of the early research was funded by the agency that also ran Los Alamos and the Nevada Test Site. And accidents still occur. Within days after the Chernobyl nuclear power plant burned, lichens around the Northern Hemisphere had absorbed giant doses of radionuclides, doing themselves no harm. But in the Arctic these plants provide the chief food of caribou and reindeer, and caribou and reindeer are important food for indigenous people. As they rise through the food chain, radionuclides become more concentrated, and the Saami people of Norway found themselves contaminated with, for instance, cesium 137 levels up to 165 times higher than normal—and with a deeply damaged cultural economy.

Even here, on this windy ridge half a globe away from Chernobyl and nearly forty years after most atmospheric bomb testing stopped, the right instruments would doubtless have revealed more radioactivity in the lichens around me than I wanted to think about. The same would have been true of the small patches soon to form of what hikers call watermelon snow. Since I first noticed its pretty color in the 1960s, I'd known it was a bad idea to eat this snow; I'd heard it would cause stomach problems. But the result might have been much worse, since the fruity scent and pale pink hue come from one of several algal species that collect and concentrate wind-dropped radioactive dust. Then, when the snow melts, these algae end up in the rivulets that drain the tundra. These days it's mostly naturally occurring radionuclides they concentrate, and the most dangerous pollutants from earlier years have settled into the bottoms of streams and rivers downhill.

None of these complications is visible to a tundra visitor, though, and that June I saw neither the troubling nor the heartening details that I later learned are so tightly woven together. What I did notice, what I have always noticed, is something much more obvious and purely pleasurable—the lichens' textures, patterns, and colors. If I could, I'd design a line of fabrics based especially on their colors: nubbly wools and fleeces in coffee and tobacco, smooth cottons in rust and charcoal, raw silks of sagebrush and parrot green, gauzy clouds of charcoal and silver, shiny synthetics in neon chartreuse and orange. And then I'd branch out into tundra flower colors, just so I could wear clothes the intense blue of alpine forget-me-nots, my favorite wildflower of all.

By the time I returned to Trail Ridge less than a week after Ptarmigan Day, when I lay on the ground and discovered such a complex miniature landscape, much of the tundra was covered with forget-me-nots in bloom. Still, if I hadn't learned long ago how to spot them, I might have missed them entirely—even when they're abundant and in full flower, they're so tiny they can disappear from a casual glance.

You might say that forget-me-nots huddle against the ground with their arms wrapped tightly around themselves for warmth. The one I studied with my magnifying glass—"my" flower—clung close to the earth, as I did, safe within a boundary layer of still air that sheltered it from the wind and would keep daytime summer temperatures some twenty degrees warmer than just a few inches higher up. It grew densely, too, the outer parts sheltering the inner, each leaf, like my own layers of clothing, making a shield for the next. A central cluster less than two inches across, a handful of satellites linked by stems that had taken root themselves, maybe four inches at its widest point: even a plant this small might have been decades old—speedy growth compared to lichens, but still slow by human measures. Its frequent neighbor dwarf clover, I read in one book, grows no more than four leaves each summer yet still qualifies as an "aggressive invader of bare ground."

I could see no green on my flower's stems or leaves, just a thick sweater of wavy white hairs, silver in the scudding sunlight. These filaments would trap heat and moisture, deflect wind, and block ultraviolet rays. Though the average annual precipitation is twenty-five inches, most of it falls as snow, and where the wind blows hardest, the ground stays mostly dry. Thus many flowering plants on the tundra are furry, though not often quite as furry as this one was, while many others have fleshy, waxy leaves, two means to the same end, protection against environmental bad news.

Forget-me-nots favor one of the toughest and driest microhabitats, the very rocky alpine meadows called fellfields. Except for a lichen or two that floats free of any attachment, plants here must be well anchored by roots either wide or deep. In the Alpine Visitor Center just up the road from Poetry Curve, I'd gazed into a glass case at another diminutive flower whose taproot was six feet long, and everywhere under the surface of the tundra, everywhere beneath my stretched-out body, grew complex mazes of roots, space to store carbohydrates over the winter to power the next year's flowering and growth. Like virtually all its neighbors, my forget-me-not was a perennial, able to pace its activities to last over several seasons. Even more efficiently than most, it would have formed leaves, shoots, and buds late the summer before, then kept them alive over the winter, for a head start on this summer's flowers.

And such flowers! Under conditions this harsh one might

expect a sturdy sort of blossom, something with muscle and sinew, a floral workhorse. But these forget-me-not blossoms were delicate and tiny, maybe a quarter inch across, fully open. They had five rounded petals, and at the center, marked by a fine circle of bright yellow, a deep black funnel collected warmth for the stamens and pistils, tiny parts I couldn't find even with my magnifying glass. I knew these blossoms were as small as their lowland cousins, but as they always do, they seemed larger and more emphatic, partly because the scale here was entirely different, foreground reduced and background expanded, but mainly because they were so saturated with pigment. Lowland blossoms, in comparison, might have been soaked in bleach. It was hard to believe anything could be so blue—not far from the cobalt of old glass Noxema jars, but velvety and incandescent like the sky on those winter evenings when the air turns purple and the atmosphere seems the size of the universe. This plant looked like the night sky in reverse: a shining silver ground with a random scattering of brilliant blue flames.

Sometime later, in a lighthearted moment, I thought about what these plants might have said to me about survival. Suppose the lichens were to whisper in my left ear and the forget-me-nots in my right. *Be patient,* they would surely counsel in unison. *Move slowly and keep a low profile. Find a space you don't have to fight for. Think ahead, conserve your resources.* In my left ear: *Accept that the same thin skin that admits nourishment also makes you vulnerable. Remember that strength depends on cooperation. Share pieces of yourself with the world.* In my right: *Knit yourself a warm sweater, a safe, calm space just your size. Put down deep roots. Be passionate. Make beauty. Bloom like mad.* And together again: *Gather your energy from the ground, the snow, the sun.*

Of course I wasn't a plant, and if I were to put down deep roots or share bits of myself with the world, it could only be metaphorically. What about the other mammals on the tundra? What advice might they have offered to me, their closer kin?

On that sunny, chilly Ptarmigan Day, I was pretty sure there were no bighorn sheep and no elk around me, though they may stay this high through quite harsh weather and would return soon enough from their wintering grounds lower down. Nevertheless, familiar animals were hidden all around me, smaller ones that spend their whole lives in the tundra, each one with its own repertoire of ingenious strategies for surviving the cold.

Pocket gophers, for instance, certainly would have been close by, though I've never seen one in the flesh. Because they live entirely underground, they barely slow down for the winter months. Instead, choosing spots where snow keeps the soil warm and soft enough to dig, they keep busy with their usual rodent routines: excavating enormous mazes of tunnels and eating their way through a supermarket of nutritious roots. They shovel the dirt out of their way and dump it in empty tunnels in the snow.

If I had thought to look, I would have found some of their eskers, long, snaky tubes of dirt named for their resemblance to the much larger Arctic eskers, tracks of vanished rivers running under vanished ice sheets. Pocket gophers are small, about the length of my hand and the weight of two ordinary chicken eggs, but they're so good at their jobs that one animal might move an astonishing *ton* of dirt over a single winter. Evidently this lifestyle suits them perfectly. To me, though, it sounds grimly familiar, a match for my most tedious inside days: incessant digging in the dark, a face full of dirt, tunnel vision.

I prefer the example of pikas, pint-sized rabbit cousins that live their lives on, in, and under the tundra's many rock piles. When I spot them during the summer, I always want to laugh both at their appearance and at their behavior. They look like toys, like furry little beanbags with miniature cookie halves for ears. As I stand still to watch, they'll zip around at top speed, pause now and then to take in the view, check to see whether I'm going to pose a danger, and utter piercing squeaks to announce their presence and claim their territories.

When I've seen them in late July or August, they've usually sported great leafy mustaches and beards—sheaves of vegetation they've cut and are carrying in their mouths to giant piles stashed somewhere among the rocks. They will have filled their pantries by the time winter sets in, and then they will move indoors. During the coldest spells they slow down some, but they stay awake and alert, and on occasion, when it's warmer and calmer, they'll venture outdoors for some clean air and sunshine, maybe a bit of adventure, a fresh perspective.

Perhaps on that June day, while I perched on my slice of granite to look around and wait for Ken to return, a pika was watching me from its own matching rock nearby. The same might have been true of a short-tailed weasel or ermine, an animal even better adapted to staying active during the winter than the pika.

These vigorous and solitary little hunters, relatives of minks and wolverines, are as comfortable beneath the ground as above it, as agile and energetic in the space that stays open between soil and snow as among summer-warmed rocks. Long, thin, and graceful, with strong muscles and jaws of legendary vigor, they are shaped for agility, diving into narrow tunnels and rock piles as smoothly as a dolphin moves through water.

In the summer their fur is brown and cream. In the winter, though, like the ptarmigan we were looking for, they turn pure white, save a black tip on their tails: each weasel transforms itself into an ermine. Why? I want to say for beauty's sake. But there are more pragmatic speculations as well, guesses about how these winter coats might offer some evolutionary advantages. In other locations, for instance, where larger predators share their winter space, their white fur may help them disappear from view while the black tip tricks attackers into taking a bite of nothing. Whiteness may add to the weasels' hunting efficiency, too, by hiding them from their own potential prey, especially on the snow's surface. And, though biologists seem to disagree about this, it may help keep them warmer by channeling heat to their skin, an important factor for such a skinny little creature. (One might be some ten inches long but weigh only as much as a single chicken egg.)

Short-tailed weasels are much more elusive than their burrowing or beanbag neighbors, though, and I've never seen one. Even the stuffed specimen at the visitor center up the road from Poetry Curve, I've heard, is actually a long-tailed weasel, mislabeled. Nor have I come across their tracks or a bleached skull—at least not that I've recognized. So this animal I have only read about and imagined, this snow ghost, this phantom of the tundra: if I didn't believe my field guides, I might think it was a myth—not a yeti or Bigfoot, but Littlefoot. And Littlefoot's advice for dealing with the blues? Perhaps it wouldn't be far from the plan I had made for myself this dark season: Put on a warm, pretty coat, go outdoors, and explore.

As I learned more about the winter ecology of small

mammals, though, it wasn't the pocket gopher, pika, or weasel that most engaged my imagination, despite their success in staying alert and active throughout the year—and despite their clear (though inadvertent) success in amusing me, in pulling me away from brooding. Instead I found myself entranced by yellow-bellied marmots.

Certainly marmots were around me while I sat still on Poetry Curve, settled in, finally, to the clarity and openness of the moment, my breath again steady, my body temperature in a reasonable balance with the air and wind. Hiking up here on the tundra on sunny summer afternoons, I had often watched these fat, furry members of the squirrel family doing much what I was doing while I waited for Ken: basking in the warmth, generally on a smooth slab of rock that provided them a particularly big view. Once, as John and I were finishing our lunch on the next ridge to the east, an especially adventuresome character had come right up to us, nose twitching, eyes shining, probably hoping for a handout, though when he started to nibble my boot, I jumped and scared him off. (Later we had named one of our new puppies after him—and sure enough, our dachshund Marmot grew to love high places, the backs of couches, the low limbs of apple trees, the top of the picnic table, where he lies in the sun and watches our backyard world. We had named his brother after a long-tailed weasel we'd met on another occasion, and yes, Weasel was thinner, his face more pointed, his leaps more sinuous, his favorite spaces underneath snug covers.) Today, though, so early in the season, would the Trail Ridge marmots still have been underground, hiding in their winter homes? Or did I just not see any because I wasn't paying the right kind of attention?

Marmots are right on the dividing line of size, too big to

keep active underground or under the snow, too short in the leg to travel downhill. (An average male might stretch out to two feet, about a third of it tail, and weigh in at perhaps ten pounds; females are smaller.) They cope instead by retreating into profound inactivity—no Orlando or Sun City for them, but a long season curled up on the couch with the curtains closed and the lights out. In the late summer they eat and eat, until they look nearly spherical trundling across piles of licheny rocks. Then they laze around, avoiding exercise. They've got a good excuse for their gluttony and sloth: they're gathering fuel, in the form of body fat, for seven or eight months.

Sometime in September or October, they go into underground retreat. Nobody really knows what these spaces look like, since they're always hidden from us—a system of tunnels, nests of cropped vegetation, separate areas for different functions. They're called hibernacula—a good word for Poetry Curve, this bit of scientific Latin, the way it evokes the serenity and bookishness of medieval monasteries. When a marmot is ready to rest, its nest prepared and the time somehow right, it curls into a tight ball with its nose buried in its fur. Such a perfect sphere of repose: I want this, too, sometimes, in my darkest times—my own hibernaculum, where I might sleep and read and daydream, protected until summer comes again.

But marmots do what no human can do. They put themselves into cold storage. Their heartbeats slow from around 120 a minute to only 8, their body temperatures drop from about the same as ours to just a little above freezing, and they completely stop eating. For many months, they'll live entirely off their summer fat, doing without any protein or green vegetables, and by the time they see the sun again, they'll have lost half their body mass.

Are they asleep? This turns out to be a complicated question, as I found out months later when I walked across campus to talk to my university's marmot man, Greg Florant. "Tell me about marmots," I asked. "I especially want to know how they survive the winters. What do they *do* down there in their tunnels for all those months?"

He laughed. "What we usually say is that they read a book."

I was startled by this joke, how well it complemented my own imaginings—and so I started wondering what kinds of books a marmot might enjoy. Something long and complex like *Anna Karenina,* maybe, for those slow, dark months. Books set in cold places, *Smilla's Sense of Snow,* perhaps, or *Frankenstein,* a novel inspired by an especially wintery summer Mary Shelley spent at the foot of a large glacier in the Alps, one that ends with the scientist and his lonely creation wandering across the Arctic ice. Maybe a literature of summer would be best, a reminder of July's abundance, something full of yearning and praise, poetry by Wordsworth or Hopkins. Or, it could be, a marmot with a factual turn of mind would choose natural history, maybe an herbal encyclopedia or a field guide to edible plants.

Then I remembered to pay attention. Greg was saying something about how marmots sleep. "But wait," I said, remembering that this was a man used to talking to nonscientists, including the newspaper reporters who call him late every January to ask what's new with these animals and their more famous lowland kin, groundhogs. "They don't really *sleep,* do they? Isn't hibernation completely different?"

Well, yes and no, he answered. When marmots are sliding into torpor, their brain activity does match that of ordinary deep sleep, or what biologists call SWS, for slow-wave sleep.

(When they get cold enough, though, down to twenty degrees, their brains slow down so much that on an EEG the animals look dead—in a state you might call suspended animation.) But they don't seem to experience REM (rapid eye movement) sleep, the time when dreams occur. Greg called this paradoxical sleep, PS, because in some ways (such as its lively brain waves) it resembles being awake. I scribbled in my notebook, surprised again by how evocative, how poetic, such stray words and facts can seem, how they can reverberate far beyond their immediate meanings. *Paradoxical sleep.*

What did it really mean to be asleep, to be awake, to be, somehow, both at once? And was everything a paradox, nothing simple or singular? But I'd have to think about this later. Now I asked, "What about arousal? I've read that they wake up every now and then. Why? How often? How long does it take to come out of dormancy, and how long do they stay alert? And what do they do *then?*"

Greg's face lit up. I'd asked the right questions: he was just writing up some results of his research on these very mysteries. He turned his computer screen so I could see it. "Here's a graph I'm working on. This data comes from marmots in the field—not in our lab." It was body temperatures over time—horizontal lines marking periods of deep torpor, sharp vertical peaks registering a dramatic rise as the animals woke up—and it made a picture even I could read practically at a glance.

Now and then throughout the winter, every two weeks or so, a hibernating marmot will wake for a while, then subside back into torpor. This arousal process is laborious and costly, requiring nearly 90 percent of the energy they'll use all winter—for just about twelve hours of alertness, they spend ten hours coming out of torpor and even longer going back in. To meet these extra demands, Greg explained, they have a particularly effective energy source called BAT—short for brown adipose tissue, which we humans have, too, but only as infants. BAT is home to lots of extra mitochondria, the body's miniature furnaces, and its interior fires allow a more efficient transformation of fat into heat. How efficiently an individual marmot manages seems to have to do with the kinds of fat in its summer diet, and this relationship was one of the things Greg was trying to find out.

What do they do when they're alert? Not much. They get rid of some body wastes, check that their burrows are still tightly sealed. But they don't eat anything, and they don't go outside. "Do they sleep?" I asked. I'd gathered that some other hibernating animals do this; I'd read that this may be one reason for arousal, to deal with sleep deprivation, or, especially, REM deprivation.

I'd been thinking about this possibility, remembering that book I'd found the summer before with its wonderful statement that nearly all mammals dream. Now that I was considering the question more critically, I supposed that this claim was based on the fact that we all experience REM sleep. And a line of poetry had been running through my head for weeks, part of a villanelle by Theodore Roethke, "I wake to sleep, and take my waking slow." I really wanted Greg's answer to be yes. But it wasn't. No, he said, yellow-bellied marmots don't arouse to sleep. We don't really know why they arouse, and we don't know if they dream. We can't ask them.

Of course he was right. No matter how intense my imaginings, I could never know the truth of a marmot's dreaming, the emotional landscapes of its life, how the world felt from inside its particular body. Instead—and I was beginning to think this wasn't much of a loss, maybe even no loss at all—I'd have to savor the mysteries and make do with the facts.

Even when the facts fell short of desire. All these clever mechanisms don't make hibernation a perfect system. Winter exacts a heavy toll, and lots of marmots don't last until spring. (Winter kills more marmots than predators do, Greg told me.) Still, they all go into the fall as if they'll certainly make it through the cold, and come late spring, sometime in April or May, the survivors emerge, raring to go and ready to breed.

On this Ptarmigan Day in early June, the Trail Ridge marmots were surely out of hibernation. Perhaps they were in their burrows napping, dreaming, curled up in warm balls, waiting for new green food, for balmier weather. Or maybe they watched me as I sat on my small slab of rock and daydreamed. Maybe they watched my classmates talk to each other on the trail above me, watched Ken climb back up the steep hill towards us. The ptarmigan he'd been following had vanished into the trees below. "There's another spot just over there we'll try next," Ken said once we had all gathered again on the trail, and so we walked to the south, past the cars and along the road to an even steeper slope where more snow had melted away. "Wait here," he directed us just before he took off downhill again. "If I capture one, you can come down then."

In no time, it seemed, my classmates and I were huddled around Ken, kneeling and sitting on a cold, wet patch of bare ground, watching him handle a bird with careful assurance. He'd caught this one with little trouble: because white-tailed ptarmigan evolved where there were few large mammalian predators, they're generally unwary of humans. Of course, before you can get close to them, you first have to see them; that's the hard part and the reason for the tape recorder. When the bird responded to the recording, Ken had walked quietly toward it, then lowered the noose at the end of his fishing pole carefully over its head. He'd slowly tightened it until he could draw the bird to him, and since they tend to freeze when something unusual happens nearby, it hadn't struggled to escape and thus was unharmed. This was a new bird, still unbanded, not yet entered into his roster of Trail Ridge inhabitants, so there were measurements to be made, notes to be taken.

Ken shrugged off his pack and opened it. He turned the bird in his hands and looked at it carefully, reminding us as he worked of what he'd covered in the morning's lecture. Sex? Female: easy to tell just now, when only the females are in full summer plumage. Age? He straightened out a wing and measured its primary feathers: two years old. Weight? Out came a small scale: just about twelve ounces, the same as a city pigeon. He clipped on the set of expanding plastic bands that would identify this individual bird, two on each leg, each a different color. All this he recorded in his notebook, part of the database he'd been building for more than two decades.

This was a beautiful bird. Her feathers perfectly matched the landscape around us, on this day caught between seasons—her body the mottled browns, blacks, and creams of spring, the colors of lichen, rocks, and matted tundra grasses, her wings and tail the clear white of the winter's snow. Her eyes were black, shiny, intense, each arched over with a thin red line like an eyebrow. Hidden inside her chest would be an extralarge heart, expanded and strengthened to deal with the demands of a life spent entirely at high altitudes where oxygen is scarce.

By now, she would have spent nearly a month on this hillside getting ready to breed, devoting up to two-thirds of every day to foraging and eating: it takes a lot of protein to make a whole new set of feathers and then lay eggs. As the summer arrives, ptarmigan shift their diet away from willow, their staple during most of the year. They look for new greens of all kinds and especially for new and highly nutritious flowers, and with eyes sharper than mine and a much more focused need, they find them. Then they snip the blossoms right off.

Imagine! A menu of summer flowers, something new every few days—one morning an anemone purée or buttercup bisque, later a salad of cinquefoil and alpine avens, in August a brochette of bistort bulblets or an alpine dryad casserole. Maybe, sometime soon, an appetizer of tiny forget-me-nots. They must taste of the season's intensity, of sun, wind, and earth.

Less than two weeks from now, the bird in Ken's hands would be sitting on her nest, somewhere on the ground where the snow had melted, hidden from the wind against a rock or at the edge of a willow patch. She'd lay six or seven eggs. Then, for the next twenty-three days, she'd leave them only to feed, at dawn and dusk. She'd sit so tightly and be so well camouflaged that a hunting weasel might pass right by and never see her. Still, nearly half of all nests are lost to predators, and with such a short season, few ptarmigan manage to lay a second batch of eggs. After her chicks hatch in mid-July, she'd guard them closely, too, especially through their first, riskiest month. The three or four that made it to fall would likely have a long life, maybe as many as a dozen years.

Ken was finished with his measurements, and now it was our turn. He explained how to hold her, firmly but gently, by her lower legs, so that she couldn't take the jump she'd need to fly. We wouldn't be hurting her, he promised; her heart rate would have risen only a little, and when we let her go, she would simply fly a few feet and get back to her meal. Then he handed the ptarmigan to the woman on his left. I watched her face: intent, a little scared, a flash of surprise as the bird stretched her wings, then delight.

Sometimes the world paints its canvas with the indifference of an axe or a blowtorch, lopping off whole branches of life with a single blow, incinerating vast landscapes in an instant. I'd been bent under the weight of this story, the long, tragic saga of extinction. But I was beginning to comprehend how evolution always follows with her intricate creative brush, a point as fine as a single hair, her unequaled attention to detail, her endless inventiveness, new ideas to try, minute changes to make, an extra mitochondrion here, a curling white filament there. Even in this hard, spare place so recently buried under ice, a landscape I imagined might resemble the aftermath of cataclysm. And, I thought now, even at the worst moments in the earth's long history, when some massive disaster had brought an end to life on an unimaginable scale, something intricate and beautiful had surely been happening, as it would happen again.

I'd known that these lovely birds changed their plumage for winter and stayed high in the mountains, but I'd had no idea until today just how thoroughly they were adapted to what I would usually think of as harsh conditions. *Adapted:* the word is precise, but we use it so often it has lost some of its force. Ptarmigan don't just adjust their attitudes when the cold arrives. They don't even much adjust their behavior. By evolving in arctic and alpine climates, they have become what they are by virtue of surviving for countless generations in an icy world. They're made in every detail to thrive in a life of winter. If the marmot speaks of retreat and repose, of the peace to be found in seclusion or at home, then the ptarmigan's bracing lessons are all about staying engaged and active in the world, however cold or dark it might be.

As the bird made her way slowly around the small circle of careful hands and hushed voices, I remembered what I'd learned today about the likely shape of her life. And I thought about what she would do once her chicks were fledged and she could leave her nest.

In late July, his territoriality forgotten, her mate would gather with the other local males below late-lying snow somewhere farther uphill, where it's cool and moist. Soon she and her fast-growing offspring would join them. On the tundra's warmest days, if she felt too hot, she'd move into the shade or the wind, maybe take a bath in snow crystals. Or she'd pant, mouth wide open, moving the air through her neck where it could cool her blood. In late September, she would begin to change into her winter plumage. As she became whiter, she'd move to snowier areas, shifting her ground in small increments so that she could continue to match her surroundings.

Finally the ptarmigan would move to where the snow lies deep and willow bushes are abundant. Her mate would travel only a mile or so and winter with another four or five birds. She'd go farther, ten miles, twenty, even thirty. She'd winter in a larger flock of females, likely of thirty to fifty, maybe many more.

How would she spend her days? Eating. More precisely, eating the buds and twigs of willow bushes, the single highly nutritious food that would make up nearly all of her winter diet. (One of the threats these birds face is competition for willow from elk, whose populations have been exploding. Depending on where they winter, another threat can be the presence of cadmium near old mines, a toxic mineral that willows concentrate. Cadmium damages livers and makes bones grow fragile.) As Ken had put it, ptarmigan are voracious feeders. At the opposite extreme from marmots, they carry almost no body fat, and so they have to eat nearly every day to survive. She would do this so well that she'd actually gain mass during the winter, while nearly every other living creature would be losing it.

When evening fell, she would work her way into the snow until she was entirely invisible and covered with a thick layer of insulation, enough to maintain an inside temperature of twenty to thirty degrees Fahrenheit even while outside it dropped to twenty or thirty degrees below zero. On really cold days, which for a ptarmigan means below zero, cloudy, and windy, she might do the same, removing herself just for a little while from the hazards of the surface. Her main danger would be a mild season without enough snow to serve as camouflage, sleeping bag, and temporary sanctuary.

This bird knew just how to behave in the winter. Along with the tundra's other survivors, plants and animals both, she also had the right body. Like the weasel's white fur, her winter feathers would work as both camouflage and heat collectors; on chilly days, she could find a patch of sunshine, fluff herself out, and let the rays of the sun penetrate the hollow shafts and reach her skin. The feathers covering her body were double, too, each carrying a second downy branch called an aftershaft, for extra insulation. In short, she was feathered all over. Feathered nostrils would keep snow and ice from impeding her breathing. Feathered eyelids would do the same for her vision. Feathers would keep her legs warm, so much so that in the winter, when all these coats are thicker, she would look like a bird walking around on a rabbit's legs. And feathered feet and soles kept her on top of the snow, doubling the weight each foot could carry without sinking, aided by a kind of fringe that grew along the sides of her toes and her long black toenails: built-in snow-shoes.

I'd planned, of course, to be a diligent student and examine the bird we captured for all these details. But from the instant my fingers wrapped around her legs, I forgot everything practical, everything about the context of what I was doing, my desire for facts, any sense of my own body's limits, sore knee, short breath, weak eyes, the thick bundles of clothing I needed to stay outside in this weather, the dark season's sadness. I forgot myself, my self-consciousness, my separate, thinking, human self, and found instead, if only for this short moment, the immediate. *This wintery place. This ptarmigan in my hands.* As I received her from my neighbor and she felt the brief freedom of her legs, she stretched out her wings and neck, thinking to fly. But with some instinctive response, my own grasp grew quickly more certain and she settled back again.

Some of the ingredients of this moment are visible in a pair of photographs someone took of me holding the bird. As I write these paragraphs many months later, I study them to help me remember, my glasses off, the prints held close to my eyes, one, then the other, then the first.

The sky is the texture of watercolors saturating thick, wet paper, a soft liquid roil of slate blue and paler gray, snow on its way, a child's triangular mountain of cumulus along the horizon to one side. Behind my head, layers of mountains stretch to the north. The hillside plunges to the left, all but a few brown patches under a thin layer of snow with spring's distinctive texture. Just downhill is a low patch of willow, and at the bottom of the photo, in the bare grass where I am sitting on a scarlet poncho, are a few faint smears of greenish fuzz. The sun shines brilliantly on the scene, and sharp lines mark the shadows I cast on myself.

I am round with layers of bright clothes, topped with blue jeans, a turquoise jacket with its purple lining visible at the collar, my cap of pink, purple, and teal. In one photo the jacket's brand name shows, embroidered in matching thread: Marmot. Giant red sunglasses obscure my eyes. My hair sticks out in tufts around my ears, its mix of white and dark an astonishingly close match to the feathers of the ptarmigan I'm holding. I'm not wearing gloves. My right hand holds her legs, and my left hand hovers lightly over her back.

Her visible wing is slightly spread, the white primaries sharply lined, and her neck stretches out. In one photo her head turns towards me and her eye is hidden. I'm holding her low across my chest, so her back shows, and my hand, four fingers curved so that just their tips touch her feathers, so lightly. I look down at her with a goofy little grin. In the other photo, I'm holding her at shoulder level, her head in front of my chin, and she shows off her perfect profile, her eye smooth and black. There is no way to tell what she is thinking or feeling. I study my face. It is in shadow and more than half hidden. I look happy. I look absorbed, tender.

What I remember most vividly, though, no photo could reveal—that sensation of something quivering behind my ribs and in my throat. It wasn't fear or even nervousness. It was anticipation and care, that rare jump of the heart that comes with wonder, the sheer thrill of holding this wild life against my skin, muscle, nerves, bone. I could feel in my own body the bird's banked energy, her softness and light warmth. I could feel the way she gathered the seasons to a point, the long ages of ice and the fleeting summer, the quiver of her heartbeats, her big strong heart.

I was the last in the circle. When I handed the bird to Ken, he let her go. She flew a few feet away and began pecking at the ground, looking for a blossom to nibble.

III

String Games

For most of my life I have dreamed of traveling far, far away.

As a child, I'd planned to live in the wilderness of Alaska, the only place it was still possible to homestead. I'd be a hermit, happy to be free from the pressure of other people, and I'd never feel lonesome. All day I'd hike and admire nature's beauty, then at night I'd read by golden lamplight in a cozy cabin. In these visions, realism played a minor role. A second plan, I should add, involved a large house in the country, six children, and many pets of various species, and in still another I'd be a lawyer, following my father's career.

Though only the country house and two small dogs had come to pass, I had kept the idea of Alaska alive. I read dozens of books about it, consoled myself when I needed consolation with the idea of moving to Fairbanks, and spent lots of time daydreaming about endless summer days, carpets of wildflowers beneath jagged mountains, vast wildernesses, silence and solitude. When I thought about winter, I rarely wondered how

I'd adapt to the dark and cold but often pictured the Northern Lights.

I had fixed on the Brooks Range as my ideal destination and invented schemes to be flown in and left there for a month or so, with just one or two other people for company and safety. But I couldn't seem to make that trip happen. John, who prefers rainforests to tundra, wasn't interested: when I mentioned the subject, his liveliest response was "Umm." Two summers in a row, now, I'd thought I'd found other friends to go with me, but those plans had collapsed. And while I had tried to talk myself into a solo journey, the sad fact was that I simply didn't have the nerve.

So I'd signed up instead for a trip to a tiny outpost on Canada's Arctic coast called Bathurst Inlet, one run by Cloud Ridge Naturalists, whose director, Audrey Benedict, I had met and liked. I'd be going to a community in a flat part of Canada, not the wild mountains of Alaska, but I'd still be far enough north to see the midnight sun and the tundra in bloom. The small tour group would offer a workable compromise between independence and loneliness, desire and safety, and I might even satisfy in a limited way my long yearning for some kind of pure solitude. All in all, it seemed a practical, though diminished, alternative.

I'd sent in my deposit—a bit of extra income from writing and speaking—way back in the previous fall. Then my cousin Carol Ann had died, I'd buried myself in data about radioactive waste and half-lives, and I'd slipped into depression. Lately I'd been absorbed in the slow, lonely labor of arousing myself from hibernation. In the month since I'd held the ptarmigan on Trail Ridge, I'd done knee therapy, acquired new glasses, studied the alpine tundra, soaked up sunlight. During all this time I'd had no energy to spare for even the near future. Also, I really didn't want to open myself up for disappointment. So I'd done little to prepare for my journey to the Far North and kept my expectations low.

Monday, July 6.

I'm standing in the charter air office in Yellowknife, and my stomach is churning. I've come on a series of ever smaller planes to ever smaller airports, west from Denver to Salt Lake City, north to Edmonton, Alberta, where we picked up the final members of Audrey's group, then farther north to this frontier mining town, the capital of Canada's Northwest Territories. We've spent the weekend touring the town and its surroundings—taiga, muskeg, and Great Slave Lake, one of the world's largest freshwater bodies. Now we are waiting for the fourth and final leg of the trip, a charter flight 360 miles farther still to the north and a bit back east, over the interstellar spaces of the Barren Grounds to the Bathurst Inlet Lodge.

I have not been looking forward to this. Following Audrey's instructions, I'm wearing jeans and hiking boots and carrying my warm jacket, rain gear, and insect repellent—an outfit I can only think is designed to serve if the plane should have to land suddenly in the middle of nowhere. Trudy, who at eighty something is our oldest and probably spunkiest traveler, just offered me Dramamine, and though I've never been airsick before, I took two. I've been expecting to board a Twin Otter, a two-engine plane too small for a bathroom, on account of which I have skipped my morning tea, but though I also haven't slept much the past few days, I'm too anxious to feel sleepy. Since I learned that our group included a retired pilot who'd flown himself and his wife from Boulder to Yellowknife, I've grilled him shamelessly about the Twin Otter's safety features and reliability. Ed, I'd asked, how nervous should I be about this plane? Is this the kind that crashes so often in Alaska?

Now it seems there's been a change in equipment. I sidle up to him. Ed, what kind of plane is that outside the building, the one they're loading those boxes on? A Dash 7? Do you think we're taking it? Cargo plus passengers? Isn't it far too big to land without a runway? I scrutinize his face the way I'll watch a flight attendant for flashes of surprise or fear at an odd noise or sudden bump. I'm also keeping a close eye on Audrey. Is it just my imagination, or do both of them look a tiny bit off balance, as if they are trying hard to stay calm?

To distract myself, I wander over to join a clump that has formed along one side of the room. An enormous topographic map covers the wall. A sturdy-looking guy who might be in his late thirties is standing there, talking. That's Boyd Warner, someone whispers to me—the pilot, the one who runs the air service, Glenn and Trish's son.

He's answering questions and pointing to landmarks. Here, he says, touching the largest smudge, is the Lupin gold mine. It's so big that you'll probably be able to see it from the air about an hour out if you look to your left. Now, in the summer, you can get there only by plane. In the late winter, though, convoys of huge trucks drive up and back on roads of ice. Yes, just ice. Straight over the lakes and the ground both. No, ice is only slippery when the surface layer melts, and it's too cold here for that. They do have to go very slowly, though, because their movement creates waves in the ice itself, and if they drive too fast, the waves bounce back at them and they crash.

The diamonds? You've been hearing about those, eh? Here, and here, and here. He points to smaller smudges scattered around the map. We fly the prospectors out—it's a lot of our business these days. They're finding some very rich deposits, he says: some of the tests have turned up a carat of diamonds for every pound of earth. Yes, a carat in each pound.

I've been edging closer as I listen, and finally I'm right against the wall. This map looks like none I've ever seen. I can find no road lines and no town names. Hardly any contour lines mark changes in elevation. Blue covers half the map, strings and splashes of lakes separated by long ribbons of land all the way to the Arctic Ocean. The latitude and longitude grid looks familiar, but on this map a third set of fine lines arcs smoothly to the northeast. What on earth could those be for? I wait for an opening and ask. Ah, he says, and smiles. These point to the north magnetic pole.

I've known for a long time that the geographic and magnetic poles don't coincide. The geographic poles mark the axis around which Earth rotates; by human standards, they're stable. The magnetic poles, which mark the ends of the planet's magnetic field, wander constantly over quite large areas. Because compasses work on magnetism (as opposed to GPS, or the global positioning system, which uses satellites), topographic maps for, say, the Northern Hemisphere always indicate the distance between the two north poles with a small pair of arrows somewhere in a corner, and to navigate accurately you need to adjust your compass to match.

What I learned only yesterday is that as you travel far to the south or the north, your compass will grow less and less accurate. The two poles move farther apart, relative to your position, and worse, you won't be able to adjust for the difference. Because the spot that attracts the compass needle is actually in the earth's mantle, a layer of molten rock many miles under the surface, the magnetic pole will be increasingly beneath your feet, and the needle won't be able to point you in a single clear direction. In a restaurant last night, where smaller maps were laminated onto the tables, I'd been thrilled to read this warning: "Compasses are unreliable beyond this point." If you were to stand directly over the north magnetic pole, the needle could do nothing but spin or freeze.

Boyd is saying something about how this phenomenon is why GPS is revolutionizing travel in the Far North, but I've stopped listening. I've also completely forgotten to be nervous. I'm just gazing at the enormous map and thinking, *How wonderful, how wonderful.* When you've drawn too close to the invisible center of their power, compasses can tell you nothing about where you are. I see now that we'll be flying straight towards the magnetic pole. And I know I'm hooked. I'm ready to get on that plane and go.

We are indeed boarding the Dash 7. I edge past a couple dozen seats towards the cargo space at the front, where I snag a spot in the first row, pretending it is mere chance that my closest neighbors are Ed the pilot; a man-of-many-trades named Randy, who seems to have some of the best wildlife-spotting eyes in the group; and Steve, an ice-age anthropologist who also teaches courses in glacial geology. Between us and the pilots lies a mound of duffel bags and suitcases, a mountain of boxes where I glimpse a head of lettuce, and a long ridge of lumber, an item whose significance I won't realize until later. It's not just that wood is rare and precious so far from treeline. Normally, the only way to get anything big or heavy to Bathurst Inlet is on a once-a-year boat, loaded somewhere south in late June, then unloaded in September. (One fact sheet I've seen lists July 15 as the usual date the ice pack breaks up; some years it never does, and the boat doesn't arrive at all.) The extra size of this plane has offered an unusual opportunity. And, a fact I'm exceedingly grateful to learn only *after* we land, this is the first time ever an airplane this big will make the trip. (In fact, I'll hear a year later that the experiment will last only two weeks; the next summer Audrey's group will be back on those Twin Otters.)

For a long time, we fly over wilderness. Thick forests, low hills, bright mounds of lichen-dappled bedrock. Slowly the spruce trees shrink and thin, and the tundra takes over. Without trees to disguise them, the signs of permafrost and recent glaciers are everywhere, so clear I can decipher them even with my scant knowledge. Patterned ground, where freezing and thawing have cracked the surface into a puzzle of giant polygons. Eskers, those long ropes of cobble and soil left where streams once ran under the ice. Potholes shining with meltwater. There, off to the west, is the gold mine. Farther west, beyond the curve of the earth, lies the giant Great Bear Lake, where, I'd learned in the museum in Yellowknife, at a place called Port Radium, there is a uranium mine that had helped fuel some of the first atomic bombs, the ones built at Los Alamos. Beneath us, a lace of caribou trails covers the ground. Patches of snow glint like mica in the distance, and on one big lake pack ice lingers, though the heat this summer is breaking all records.

Suddenly the pilot drops low, really low, the plane turns into a lumbering giant, tipping left and right, up and down, and my heart leaps into my throat. If we are going to crash, I know in an instant, I want to go down with my eyes wide open. The ground that has looked flat, monotonous, and mostly gray is suddenly transformed by proximity: a green crumple of hills and ravines, white waterfalls and meadows of white cotton grass, fat ropes of bedrock scraped clean by advancing glaciers and boulders left scattered when they melted.

For maybe twenty minutes we skim close over the ground, rising and falling with its contours. At last, out of all this space materializes a red and white cluster of buildings. Then a bare strip bulldozed into the tundra along the water's edge, and with only a little bump we're down. The whole community has come to meet us—and to celebrate the big plane's first landing on their newly enlarged runway.

In the afternoon, we tour the village—though the word sounds too grand for what is here. The cabins lining the shore where the Inuit live will be off-limits for us the rest of the week, but today we're taken to examine their fish racks, washing machines, a rack or two of drying caribou parts, a couple of dogs tied up and barking, snow machines parked for the season. Some of these folks live here year-round, while others spend winters where there are jobs and schools, but all, we're told, are committed to maintaining many elements of traditional Inuit life. The largest building is the old trading post, the lodge headquarters where we'll gather for meals and slide shows. There are three or four cabins for guests. The old Catholic church still stands, too, desanctified and turned into guest quarters: here, in a cubbyhole just big enough for a single bed, a tiny table for a lamp I won't need, and a small chest of drawers, is where I'll be sleeping.

By evening we've met the people on the staff we'll be talking to the most. Glenn and Trish Warner are founders of the naturalist lodge, part owners (they're partners with the extended Inuit family that makes up this community), and chiefs in charge of tourist relations. They came to the Far North forty years ago, Trish as a nurse, Glenn as a Mountie patrolling by dogsled this big empty piece of country. The little yellow Super Cub at the dock is his plane; I'll be going up with him later in the week, a part of the Cloud Ridge package I will not skip, nervous or not. Page Burt is the staff naturalist. She came here maybe twenty years back as a visitor, then abandoned her old life in Ohio and made a new one in the Northwest Territories—a move I might have made myself if a few things had happened differently. Jack Sperry, twenty years the Anglican priest at Coppermine to the west, then for twenty more the Bishop of the Arctic, now retired and living in Yellowknife, has come back north to help guide during the three-week summer season. And Doris Kingnektak, who spends most of her year a couple hours north of here in a home as isolated as it's possible to be, will come on our daily explorations as a guide. Page tells us that Doris lives by choice in an unusually traditional Inuit way, though one with a twist, as it's she who hunts to sustain her family, and though so far she hasn't said very much, I look forward to hearing her talk about her life.

Tuesday.

After breakfast, I join the other guests on a flat-bottomed boat about the size of a living room. I choose a perch along the side, then smear on sunblock and industrial-strength insect repellent. Even if spilled drops *are* rumored to eat through plastic, I've decided that a week of DEET poses a trivial risk. After all, I spent my sunburned, high-altitude childhood downwind from a nuclear bomb test site, a plutonium trigger factory, and a chemical weapons storage plant. Others have chosen to wear bug jackets, hooded anoraks of tightly woven ivory cloth and netting that render the wearers ominously faceless. (I tried one on, but it made me claustrophobic.) When the mosquitoes are especially intense, we'll look like a crew heading for Chernobyl after the meltdown.

I've also tailored for myself a cheap fisherman's vest with a pocket for each piece of equipment I might want to carry—rain jacket, sunglasses, small binoculars and camera, extra film, magnifying glass, tiny tape recorder, notebook, and pencil. I have no plans to be rigorous about using all this stuff, but these days I'm in the habit of taking notes, and sometimes the right tool for looking or recording can be liberating. I certainly don't intend to write about this trip. In fact I plan *not* to write about it. I'm giving myself only two jobs for the week: I'm going to pay attention, keep my eyes wide open and my mind alert. And I'm going to try to feel *alive.*

Finally everyone arrives on deck and, as we will do every morning, we set out to explore the inlet. The water gleams glassy blue and vast, stretched like a mirror clear to the distant low hills of the horizon. The sky—space itself, it seems—glows with the soft northern light I've read about. It's far more beautiful here than I've expected, or even hoped.

Not much happens to punctuate the serenity of the scene. A seal pops up and studies us, as curious as we are. A flight of oldsquaws, some scoters. I've never seen these birds before, but Page keeps a sharp lookout and names what we're seeing. So does Randy, the man with the good eyes, and we've got one other serious birder along, though he's being quiet about it. Page and Jack tease Doris about looking for caribou to shoot once the lodge closes for the season. Audrey's alert, too, but she's keeping a low profile, letting Page run the show; she also seems happy to have her husband, Jim, along, and they talk quietly together.

We stop first on Bird Island, a tiny bump in the water loaded with yellow flowers, gull nests, a few king eider nests, and a noisy lot of agitated birds: such beautiful eggs, such soft feathers scattered about. Later we step off the boat onto the stage of a broad, shallow amphitheater. It rises before us in steps, each curved terrace some six feet deep and a foot higher than the next, each a smooth sweep of cobbles and skipping stones. It reminds me of Utah or Arizona, all dark red rock set against bright blue.

At home, a shoreline like this would mark the dropping water levels in a reservoir during a drought. But ocean levels don't fall in times of global warming. Instead, Page says, these are rebound beaches, traces of the last ice age. The ice here lay nearly two miles thick, and when it melted, the surface of the earth bounced back in response. Elastic and buoyant in its sudden lightness, it rose more quickly than the ocean did, and sometimes, in places like this, more quickly than erosion and the soil-making actions of plants. Each new terrace marks a single deep breath, a single gesture of relief, the land shaking off the weight of winter.

Just to the left rises a homely jumble of lumpy cliffs. Page is saying something about algal limestone, but I'm thinking about rebound beaches and not really listening to her. Then, quietly, Audrey tells me, "Those are stromatolites," and I snap back to attention. I've read about these fossils, I even drew one on my history-of-the-world time line, but I have certainly never expected to see any. These are well over a billion years old (one visiting geologist said 2.7), formed when this piece of the North American plate—the Canadian Shield, the oldest core of the continent—floated near the equator. In warm, shallow waters, likely near volcanic vents, cyanobacteria amassed into pillow-shaped mounds. Some were hand-sized, others as big as double beds or small rooms. Some of the very earliest living things on Earth, they absorbed sunlight, exhaled oxygen, and jump-started the atmosphere necessary for life on land. When each sheet filled with silt, another grew on top, as pearls form one skin at a time. The result was this complex maze of stone, intricate curving laminations of tans and browns, each layer paper-thin, sharp-edged, and sinuous.

Loose pieces lie everywhere, and so I pick up a few to study and keep. I walk out alone onto a rebound terrace and sit on one fresh layer of earth with my feet on an even newer one, miniature flowers and bright lichens to my sides. In my hand I hold a chunk of ancient life, round and sandpapery on one side, a rough slice of swirling onion on the other, miniature dunes and terraces and wave marks, crosscuts tracing small catastrophes, the disasters of an hour or a day.

Only a couple of years ago, before I started reading about geology and the history of life, I would have seen nothing remarkable here. Now, though, I find myself imagining I'm on the set of a nature documentary. It might be titled *Our Living Planet,* and I might be speaking to the camera: "Here, with these two geological formations, we see the very old and the very new, the Tropics and the Arctic, summer and winter. . . ." I stroke the raspy surface of the stromatolite. The swirls on my own fingertips echo its lines. How can I comprehend this place, even find words for it? It's *ironic,* I think, this juxtaposition, or maybe *paradoxical*—as if such human words could apply to stone, rather than to my own limited understanding.

Maybe it's the strain of trying to stretch my mind so far, or maybe there's an undiscovered kind of magnetism at work here, but I'm feeling poised somewhere between waking and dreaming. It's as if these rocks were pulling me into a liminal space beyond geology.

Wednesday.

This morning we float across the inlet for a while, then split into two groups. One will hike to a waterfall and hope to find musk oxen, the option I'd probably choose if I hadn't just had that trouble with my knee. The other group will look at traces of the long human occupation of this area—old stone tent rings, meat caches, game drives, traps, and hunting blinds. Our small group includes three archaeologists—one amateur, Jack Sperry, and two professionals, Steve Cassells and Jim Benedict—and it doesn't take me long to realize that I can learn a lot if I shadow them, try to mimic their vision, and listen to them as they imagine the past.

Tall, lanky, rumpled Jack takes charge and leads us from site to site. I've already been charmed by this man. I love his title— Bishop of the Arctic!—and how casually he points to the enormous territory he covered when he was the priest at Coppermine. He moved here from England as a young man, not long after serving with the British navy in World War II, so I suppose he is close to my father's age. He has translated parts of the New Testament into Inuktitut, which he seems to speak with some fluency. And he brings to my mind all the people who have come as outsiders to the Arctic and fallen under its spell.

He seems serene to me, Jack does, and he's witty, too. He's also packed with information and stories, so I've been listening whenever he mentions something about his life up here. How he built a freezer of ice blocks for his house in Coppermine so his wife and children would eat well when he was gone. How full of fears and taboos some of the people here used to be, how once he found a family starving to death yet refusing to eat some food they considered forbidden, and how confidently he believes that Christianity has been, on the whole, a force for good up here. How he used to travel by dogsled to visit his parishioners—a day's hard journey over snow and ice to one family or small group, two days more to the next, out six weeks at a time in the cold, sunny days of spring or the moonlit days of winter. Three thousand miles a year by dogsled, at about four miles an hour: That's a lot of time for thinking, he says. I wonder what those journeys required—and what they taught—of fortitude, faith, and commitment.

Now he leans on his walking stick and speculates about each stone structure we stop to admire. Many of the stones are coated with lichens that take centuries to grow; others look almost as clean as if they had been moved just last year. That trap would have caught foxes, this one something larger, wolves or wolverines. This tent ring would have been for summer, set high in the wind to keep the mosquitoes away. That one, see how it's sheltered by the cliff? It would have been used in winter. Steve and Jim chime in, drawing on what they've learned excavating similar hunting structures high in the Colorado Rockies.

Jack leads us to a terrace holding several summer tent rings. Jim—thin as grass, soft-spoken and kindly, grizzled by high-altitude sun—wanders to the side, stops in an undistinguished spot, and says, "Here's a toolmaking site." He leans over and picks up a rock. It's red, oval, palm-sized, sharpened at one end into an edge for scraping skins or bones. "How on earth can you tell that's not just an ordinary rock?" I ask. He pulls out his magnifying glass and shows me the chip marks, but I can hardly see them, they are so subtle and worn. He squats again and says, "Here's a knife." This one is the shape and size of my little finger, with tiny scallops up one side. He sets a dime next to it for scale and takes a photo. "And over here are some of the chips they knocked off." It might take ten of these fragments to cover that dime, but to Jim's experienced eyes, their color and shape are, apparently, obvious.

Another day we'll stand quietly a few feet away from a human grave. As was usual before Christianity took hold here, the body had simply been placed on the surface of the ground, along with some prized possessions for the spirit's next world. A metal cup and old rifle lie weathering with the scattered bones. "We think this must have been a man," Jack says, "because of the rifle. That would have been a very valuable possession indeed." Jim asks Steve what he thinks—they're old friends, so Jim knows that Steve occasionally does some forensic anthropology. He looks for a minute. Then he says, "Well, that skull doesn't have a brow ridge, which it should if it were a man's." He pauses. "The bone along the sides is thicker than usual, which is typically male. But women can have it in cultures where they carry heavy loads with tumplines." He takes a step to the side and looks some more. "That pelvic bone is definitely female. But that tibia isn't human. It's probably caribou." What a tale this must have been, visible now only in these silent traces. In the culture this woman lived in, hunting was a man's job. Did she do it anyway, stretching beyond the usual bounds, as Doris does now? If so, did she hunt because she was skillful, sharp of eye and steady of aim, or because she loved the solitary challenge, or because her survival required it? Or was the rifle a tribute, a final gift from her husband, perhaps, a sign of love or grief?

*T*his evening, it's Glenn's turn for a talk and slide show. He has some great stories to tell about dogsledding, and also about something I should probably already know of but don't, the Distant Early Warning, or DEW, line. When Glenn started to work up here as a policeman in the mid-fifties, the United States was rushing to build a radar site every fifty miles along the coasts of Alaska, Canada, and Greenland, aiming to detect manned bombers coming over the Pole from the USSR. After a couple of days crossing empty country, Glenn and his dogs would suddenly find themselves eating steak and salad with a crew of lonesome Yankees. People worry now about the PCBs from the transformers and the lead paint they used, he says, but in those days all anybody thought about was building that line before we really needed it.

In bed, I lie awake for a long time, thinking. I'm doing this every night. No matter how tired I know I must be, I'm just too excited to feel sleepy. Every few minutes, I reach up to pull aside the curtain and marvel again at the sky, still light blue even in the middle of the night. "Oh, cool," I murmur, elated to be so far north in midsummer, where so much seems new and wonderful.

*L*ater, I watch the moon rise. It is just a day past full, so I've calculated that it should appear around one in the morning and I've set my alarm. When I wake abruptly around twelve-thirty, I pull jeans and a mosquito jacket over my pajamas and walk as quietly as I can out of the creaky old church.

Smoky maroon clouds are smeared across the north, where the sun has dipped behind low hills. Higher up, the sky looks blue but oddly flat, as though pigment had replaced light. The tundra seems hollow, too, and the wind blows as if the planet were spinning momentarily out of control. I walk carefully up the long slope towards the fragile white wooden crosses of the tiny graveyard, through a landscape that seems entirely strange. There's a fresh grave here, with a pack of cigarettes lying on the ground. It belongs to a young man who killed himself a few months ago; Jack performed a service for him just last week. Another young man drowned over the winter, but I don't readily see a marker for him, and I don't want to intrude on this space to look more closely.

I've thought a lot, lately, about solitude. As a word, a condition, a concept, in what it enables and what it precludes, solitude suggests so many tensions, so many desires and fears. Privacy. Self-sufficiency, independence. Isolation and loneliness. Contemplation. Dependency, community. Exile. Relationship, intimacy. Symbiosis. Cooperation, competition. These things churn around in my head, usually as a steady undercurrent, but sometimes they rise to the surface and I find myself caught in their tangles.

All year, I've yearned for solitude and found plenty of it. Yet I've also been profoundly lonely. I've struggled with myself to understand this feeling. I've wondered whether it's simply been a symptom of depression, or worse, the fruit of some failure in generosity. And I've wondered whether I might be experiencing what some call an essential and unalterable fact of living, that we're all truly alone, always. Yet mostly I've felt as if I were sensing a pervasive condition of my place, my culture, and even more basically, my own particular span of Earth time, as if I were sensing a profound rending of the fabric of the world. Despite what we may wish or fear to think, the world isn't made up of isolated individuals. It's all webs and networks, we're all knotted together, and like it or not, every grief is a blow to all of us. I have read somewhere that the biologist E. O. Wilson has called ours the Age of Loneliness, because we're facing the extinction of so many fellow creatures, and I've thought, *Yes, that's what I'm sensing, that's it exactly.*

I look downhill to the community buildings and see no sign that anybody else is awake. I'll probably never again stand alone in so remote a place, I think. I might as well have the whole globe to myself. Though the scene is definitely eerie, I realize I'm not at all frightened, then wonder how I do feel. Lonely? I suppose so, but to my own surprise, I truly don't *mind.* I feel as if I'm poised in some kind of pure solitude. The cords holding me to the world have stretched into fine threads, but they are still holding me safe.

After a while, the moon rises up out of the tundra directly to the south, giant, white, and glowing with all the light lost from the rest of the scene. It floats just high enough to show its full circle, hangs motionless for an uncanny moment, then sinks again in the same place.

*T*hursday.

This morning I'm scheduled for my hourlong flight with Glenn. As the boat pulls away, I'm clambering gracelessly onto the wing strut and into the minuscule backseat of the Super Cub. I buckle in, put on the headphones Glenn hands me, and resolutely disregard my qualms. I've taken another of Trudy's Dramamine pills and decided this would be a pretty good way to die.

We scoot across the water for a bit, then float into the sky. Through the headphones Glenn says reassuring things. He lists the emergency supplies crammed into the tiny cargo space behind me, then points out that careless pilots don't get to be as old as he is. I snap a photo of the community, before its two dozen small buildings shrink and disappear.

Just a few minutes into the flight, I realize that I absolutely love what I'm doing.

We cross some water, then some land. I take two pictures of caribou trails—amazing how sharply drawn they are. One shot of a distant waterfall. I try out the binoculars, but the plane's vibrations interfere. Then I decide both gadgets are distracting me and put them away.

Glenn starts pointing things out to me. Two brilliant dots of white on the lake below: tundra swans, nesting. A flutter of white-fronted geese. A long stretch of tundra. From this height, it seems uninhabited, but of course it isn't.

Caribou, he exclaims. Straight down, a pair of them. I see one, pale tan and moving fast. But where's the other? It's not as though there's anywhere for a large animal to hide. Glenn loops the plane around and a second caribou materializes. This one is dark brown, and it's right next to the first, hidden from me only by my excitement and untrained eye. Under the noise of the plane, the two caribou spin around each other in a tight circle, the dark coat of summer and the pale coat of winter.

Suddenly the plane begins to bump, and I see we're heading straight towards a giant black wall of rain. Sorry, Glenn says, but we'd better turn back. We'll try again another day.

We spend this rainy afternoon in the lodge seeing more slides and listening to more stories. By now I've learned how every visible landscape is also thickly layered with invisible ones, and my picture of this place is filling in. In all its apparent simplicity, it offers a tidy microcosm of much that has happened and is happening now across the Arctic. It's just a matter of following the connecting lines.

From the Hudson's Bay Company building we sit in, lines lead to European exploration and the fur trade, forces that brought the rest of the world and its economic systems to the Inuit, for good and for evil. From Glenn Warner, they go to Canadian law and governmental policy, to the way air travel truly opened the North to outsiders, to the U.S. military influence, to the effects felt even here of the Cold War. From Trish Warner, to the government's efforts, some more successful than others, to maintain the health of its indigenous citizens. From the family expediting service, their son Boyd's operation in Yellowknife, to the past and future of mineral exploration and mining—gold, uranium, diamonds.

From Jack Sperry and the church where I sleep, lines reach to the complicated influence of Christian missionaries on Inuit culture. From the joint ownership of the lodge and from Page Burt's job as a naturalist, to the contemporary importance of ecotourism. From Doris's new business as a hunting guide, to another potential source of income in this region with few paying jobs. From the Inuit families of Bathurst Inlet, the Kingaunmiut, to their own long history in the Arctic. From everyone here, the Inuit and their guests alike, to the social and medical problems that plague us all, troubles we share but usually prefer to treat as private. And from the land itself—rock, plants, animals, sky—connecting lines extend in so many directions: to continental drift, the evolution of life, long-term climate change; to PCBs in toxic concentrations, radionuclide-heavy lichens, poisoned caribou, contaminated hunters; to the ozone hole, global warming, and a polar ice cap that has begun to melt.

After all I've learned during the past couple of years, I'm no longer startled by how complex and difficult these connections are, how deep the layers, how beauty so often masks trouble, how a place even this remote will be so tightly woven into the world. What I couldn't have expected is my emotional reaction. For months I've been piling up sorrows, knitting each new one into a heavy load of grief, anger, and despair. But now, somehow, I'm managing to hold sorrow in balance with joy.

Maybe it's because I'm so saturated by sunlight. Maybe it's the kind of visitor I'm being, just going where I'm taken and absorbing what I'm told, handing myself over to the knowledge and wisdom of others, as if just for this week I were as free of responsibility and as new to the world as an infant. Maybe it's the open quality of the landscape, its slow rhythms, its subtle shapes and colors, its wide, spare, luminous spaces. Whatever the causes, in a way I'm not used to, I seem to have loosened the habit of analysis and rationality, the duty to think critically about everything. Instead, I feel content to drift, float, daydream. It's as if all the knots inside me are coming untied.

*F*riday.

The sky is clear this morning, and Glenn takes me flying again. Beneath us stretch such wide expanses, seawater, lakes, and streams, the swollen, cracked polygons of permafrost, bumpy tussocks and gullies and hills, everything flush with summer.

Today I'm beginning to understand the scale of the landscape and our distance above it, so I do a better job of seeing than I did yesterday. Mostly the tundra seems empty, but I know now that only large mammals will be visible and I'm more alert to the color patches that might signal their presence.

There, says Glenn, just by that stream. It's three musk oxen, big, dark, and shaggy. I've read about these ancient animals, and yesterday we glimpsed a distant pair, but I've never really seen one. We're close enough now that even from this height, the gesture of their thick curved horns is visible. Two lie down and one grazes, immersed in these brief balmy moments and sweet, nourishing flowers.

The next sighting is mine: a grizzly bear! We loop around. The bear looks so small, cinnamon with smooth, thick fur. It runs in a big circle, up one side of a rock outcrop, across, down, over again. We are scaring it, and so we fly on.

We cross over tundra, a river, the spectacular Wilberforce Falls where I take the day's first photo—I've been far too busy looking to bother with my camera. Glenn points to some tiny lakes where he's twice dropped people off to spend time alone, a priest in retreat and an Alaskan couple looking for wilderness. More tundra, more water. Finally the boat at anchor and a scatter of tiny human figures. We land with a low spray of saltwater, and I climb out, shaky with pleasure.

In the afternoon, we wander over a small island of ridge and rebound beaches until we reach a slender pond edged lightly with willow bushes and silver lichens. If we are careful and lucky, Page says, we might find a red-throated loon on her nest. And so we do, just below where we stand, woven into the meeting point of water and grasses. In our sudden, threatening presence, she holds absolutely motionless. Two others, more easily startled, float out on the water. Their cries are shorter and more raucous than the more familiar call of the common loon, but they, too, sound plaintive, bereft.

What is it about the loon on her nest that is so mesmerizing? I'm not the only one who finds it so: tripods and spotting scopes and a half-dozen telephoto lenses have appeared along our silent ridge. I dig out my pocket binoculars, sit so I can steady my elbows on my knees, and study her, sitting as still as I know how. I keep my breath shallow and my heartbeat slow, and I focus on this small bright circle.

She holds herself in perfect silhouette, her head tilted slightly up. Her neck is slender and graceful, her back mottled with colors picked up from the tundra. Soft gray over her face. Narrow black and white lines down the back of her neck, sharply defined and wavering like reflections in still water. Between beak and breast, a long patch of dark red, the sun itself caught in her throat. An eye the color of fresh blood, its center a tiny black hole, her gaze fixed and fierce. Everything about her seems muscular and concentrated, as though all the forces of life had come together in her body.

A little later, when we've moved to another island, a quick rainsquall blows through. I huddle beneath an old seal blubber cache, a pillar of rock streaked with hardened drippings from who knows how many years past. It looks like blackened amber, has the texture of a Tootsie-Roll, and smells sweet and smoky.

Sometime close to midnight, I go canoeing with Audrey, Jim, and Steve. The sun shines low in the northwest, and I can't stop thinking that we'd better hurry back before dark, though I know that dark won't be arriving. The boat Audrey and I share is oddly bent and hard to manage, the current and light breeze are against us, the mosquitoes buzz fiercely around our heads, and we drop slowly behind.

"Caribou!" Audrey exclaims, "Over there, ahead of us, on the right bank."

I balance my paddle and fish for my binoculars, juggle with my glasses, start scanning the area she is pointing to.

"No, not a caribou, wrong shape. Got it. It's a *wolf!* See it?"

To my surprise, I do, my aim and focus suddenly perfect. It is unmistakably a wolf. White and long-legged, it stands right on the edge of the bank some eight feet above the water, not backlit, exactly, but sidelit, and it is looking straight at us. It could have been watching us for a long time, and we might never have known. Its fur glows as if illuminated from within by a thousand candles, as if it stored within itself all the light of the summer for the dark months ahead.

After a long moment, we decide on the risk of generosity, call to Jim and Steve—too quietly for human ears, yet not quietly enough—and watch the wolf turn and disappear.

Lying awake in bed, I think about all the animals I've seen here: caribou and musk oxen, swans and loons, Barren Ground grizzlies and arctic wolves. They're the icons of the Far North, the glamour species. I suppose they might seem to me like clichés, the too familiar emblems of postcards and calendars. But they don't. Each of these animals seems to be what each one truly is, nothing more and nothing less than *real.* However magical they look, their bodies are as material as mine, as strong and as vulnerable. Like me, they live rounded and complex lives.

They also suggest qualities I don't feel are mine. They fit so perfectly into this place, their home. They seem so focused and so self-contained, out alone on the vast tundra. And so independent of human presence or absence. True, we frightened the bear and the caribou, the wolf vanished at the sound of our voices, the loon froze on her nest while we photographed and stared at her. But such minutes of human contact can occur only rarely in such a lightly populated place. Mostly, their privacy remains unbroken. Too, the musk oxen ignored us, the wolf had studied us before we spotted it, and certainly all around us other bears and caribou and wolverines, wolves and foxes and loons, have escaped even our gaze.

These creatures, I think, must live their lives almost entirely without regard to us. As Glenn reminds everyone he takes flying, you can never count on seeing any animal. In this unbounded landscape, they are where they want to be, and nowhere else. And so each appearance represents a momentary encounter between worlds, not a complete communication but an opening for the imagination, a recognition of life on a shared planet, a brief chance to see beyond my own ordinary limits.

It was the purity of their solitude that first captured my attention, I suppose, this and the way these animals seem to inhabit the summer with such intensity. And yet in glimpses so brief, I know I can only be seeing tiny slivers of their lives, a few seconds out of years. What will fill the rest of their days? I muse about this question, going over what I know from reading, trying to imagine some of the rest. After this flash of summer, what then?

In just a couple of weeks, the caribou will head south for the winter, though not so far south as to get what I'd call warm. With hooves designed for snow and a thick, warm winter coat, they'll move into the trees. There the snow will stay loose enough that they can keep digging for their food, those thick, spongy, silvery tangles of lichen that look, close up, like piles of caribou antlers. Scattered for the summer into ones and twos, for migration and the dark months they'll join a community of thousands. The loons will fly much farther, to open coastal waters farther down the continent, perhaps as far as the Everglades. A little later, the bear will slip into its den and its long winter, not in hibernation, technically, but slowed down in similar though milder ways. It might rest alone or wait out the cold with a cub or two—we could easily have missed seeing a second bear, as at first I'd missed the second caribou.

The musk oxen will stay on the tundra, gathered into larger groups for warmth and safety, perfectly adapted to the harshest weather. The wolf will remain, too, to hunt alone or with its pack. With a small handful of other creatures—willow and rock ptarmigan, foxes, wolverines—these arctic creatures will continue their lives uninterrupted, right here.

Slowly my glimpses of these wild animals are taking on weight for me. They are becoming emblems of what they reveal and what they do not show, what in fact they hide from view—the months spent not alone but in families, packs, flocks, herds; the long migratory journeys; the winters much longer than summers, endless nights of cold wind, snow, and darkness, when the full moon might circle the sky while the sun appears only to rise and set again in the same spot.

They hint at the depth and complexity of living in this place. In my imagination these fleeting visions are becoming more and more resonant and suggestive, cryptic images of balance and poise, courage and joy. They trace for me stories about how life might be lived with a steady intensity, summer without dread of winter, winter without yearning for summer, a sure and delicate balance of solitude and connection, darkness and brilliance spinning around each other like a pair of caribou, one light and the other dark, in the tight circle of a single whole.

Saturday.

Today's explorations turn into geology and botany lessons. I've recognized many of the plants from Trail Ridge, but many are unfamiliar, too. Though for a change I haven't worked at learning their names, I've been admiring them all week—they cover the ground everywhere there's soil, and they're lovely.

Reindeer lichen, loose, spongy, silvery balls of it, all mixed in with bright green horsetails, the same species, it looks like, that I'd found that wintery day in northern New Mexico, those ancient land plants that once reached the height of trees. Cotton grass. Miniature carnivorous bog flowers with leaves like squashed yellow stars. Labrador tea, cloudberry, bog rosemary. Sweet peas so fragrant that they saturate the air of whole islands. Arctic white heather, or *Cassiope tetragona*, my favorite new plant, a bizarre stack of bent tetrahedrons. All these flowers appear, bloom, and set seed in just a week or two each—and I thought the growing season on Trail Ridge was short!

*T*onight is the cultural evening, the one time we visitors are joined by the Inuit families of Bathurst Inlet, the Kingaunmiut, or People of the Nose, named for the distinctive shape of the ridge just uphill from this lodge. Much of the program revolves around a collection of tools and clothes that the lodge owners have commissioned some of the older people in the area to make for them, as a way of recording part of the material culture and artistry of the past. A few of these items are used today; some date from midcentury, when most people here lived nomadic lives based in part on the fur trade and had access to some European materials; others predate the influence of Europeans. According to Page, the Inuit in this stretch of the Arctic were the last to have contact with Europeans, not until shortly before World War I. (Early ethnographers called them the Copper Eskimos, because they had access to a local source of that metal.) It hasn't been so very long since these items were used here regularly.

First Jack and Glenn talk about the hunting and fishing tools on display around the lodge. Then Page narrates as a handful of people model outfits. She explains how wolverine fur makes the best face ruffs because it sheds ice most readily, how moose hide makes strong soles, how caribou skins were worn both fur in and fur out for layers of insulation to match the seasons. Some of these pieces are for everyday work. Others are fancier ceremonial clothes, elaborately pieced with different colors and textures of skin and fur, dangling pom-poms of bright yarn, tassels of soft white fur that once would have been weasels but here are rabbit skins.

The models look happy, but their faces are flushed and damp. Clearly these garments are *warm*. Later I pull one briefly over my head; it is heavy and smells like old meat. They are also cleverly designed to make efficient use of available materials and meet the demands of the climate. They are skillfully sewn. And they are quite beautiful.

When the clothing show is over, Martha Akoluk sits on the floor to light the heavy soapstone lamp. Children kneel beside her. These lamps were valued household possessions, carefully guarded and handed down through families. They warmed igloos enough for comfort (but not enough to melt the ceilings), they provided heat for cooking, and they gave light when the sun could not. Once the best fuel would have been rendered and pounded seal blubber, but the lard Martha is using seems to work well, too. The wick, which stretches the length of the shallow dish, is of cotton-grass seed. It takes skill to light and tend these lamps, and everyone pays close attention as Martha coaxes the flame into a narrow, steady, golden glow.

A couple of young men drum and sing and dance. Then, finally, two girls in their early teens show us some traditional string games. These aren't like the cat's cradle games I played endlessly when I was their age. Most of them require only one maker, and the results are far more artful. Once, they were permitted only in midwinter, on the days when the sun did not appear; to play them at other times was to invite cosmic trouble. But these two smiling girls don't seem a bit worried now, on this bright evening in high summer. They're old enough to be proficient with a large repertoire. Their hands blur between figures, each one quickly made and named, a kayak, a seal coming up for air, a fishing net.

Perhaps whatever understanding I've been moving toward needed to begin with lichens and a ptarmigan, the rising moon and a midnight wolf. Now, though, I'm becoming fascinated by the people who have figured out how to live here, in what must be for human bodies one of the world's most difficult environments.

These things we've been shown tonight—they go far beyond the material needs of vulnerable bodies, but I think they must be just as crucial to survival. They draw from the richness of culture, from deep sources of creativity, art, and imagination. They tend to the needs of the human spirit.

Sunday.

Jack runs a brief service this morning. Though I long ago stopped going to church, I'm interested in what he has to say.

He tells a story about John the Baptist's time in prison, how he told his followers he did not mind the dungeon's darkness because of the light he had stored inside himself. Jack says we can do this, too, as we end this extraordinary interlude and return to our ordinary lives.

With the help of a handout, we stumble through "Amazing Grace" in Inuktitut. We sing a hymn I loved as a child, too, one giving thanks for the beauty of the world, and I find myself close to tears.

Later I decide to choose a small keepsake or two from the shelf in the dining room where handmade items appear at odd intervals. I already have a few things I'm planning to take home—a couple of stromatolite shards, a caribou vertebra and one from a musk ox, both splattered with lichen, a little chunk of aged seal blubber. But I've fallen under the spell of two pencil drawings done by one of last night's string-game girls, Bella Kapolak. They portray bow hunters wearing thick skin clothing. In one, a caribou is the target; in the other, this time in colored pencils, it's a trio of geese. In both, the lines and shadows of the landscape seem exactly right. I'm also charmed by their homemade frames of cardboard and fabric, maroon trimmed with white rickrack, bright blue with gathered lace. Finally I decide I don't have to choose between them and buy both. I also buy a ring that Doris carved of caribou bone. It's a simple circle of creamy ivory bearing the tiny head of an alert-looking arctic fox, an animal I've never seen, though I believe they have been near me this week. I'm happy that this ring evokes a creature that has remained, to me, invisible.

Monday.

The plane is supposed to arrive late this morning, bringing the summer's third and final group of visitors and picking us up. But the wind is blowing so hard in Yellowknife that both the land and the water airports are closed; one floatplane, Trish has heard over the radio, flipped on takeoff. So we have an un-determined number of bonus hours to spend, a gift of bad weather.

It's windy here as well, too windy for the boat, but most of us bundle up against the chill and hike up the ridge. For a while I stay with the others, enjoying their company, but finally I wander off by myself—a pattern I've slipped into this week and find very comfortable. A solitary caribou seems to be following me.

After lunch, we hear that the plane has finally taken off in Yellowknife. We have just about two hours left, but the cold wind has tired us, and it seems a good time to retreat indoors.

I sit next to Doris on the couch. I like this young woman very much, and I'm intrigued by the little I've learned about her. Because she has come on the boat every day as a guide, I have seen much more of her than of the other members of the Inuit community, who have kept busy with their own jobs and families. I like to think about her home about two hours north by motorboat or snowmobile, how far she lives from any settlement, in a place even more isolated than this one, just a couple of small buildings alone in an immense wilderness of water and tundra. Nearby, there is another stromatolite reef and a house built from its rock many centuries ago by people of the Thule culture, ancestors to the modern Inuit.

She is some years younger than I, I'm not sure how many, and like me she has no children. She is unmarried—according to Audrey, who has known her for many years, because she likes her independence. She lives with her mother, a nephew, and a younger brother, her family reduced to a mere handful by a series of social and natural disasters. Glenn told me that she'd never gone to school. She lived too far away, and her family needed her too much; she is, in fact, their main provider. She earns some cash working at the lodge a few weeks each year and sometimes more as a hunting guide; last winter, she took a rich woman out to kill a musk ox. But mainly she keeps her family fed through her own considerable trapping and hunting skills—the furs of wolverines, foxes, and wolves, the meat of caribou by the dozens. She lives a life that speaks strongly to my imagination—outdoors all year long, skillful and self-sufficient in ways I have only dreamed of matching, thriving, it seems, on solitude. I have felt more strongly each day that I would like to apprentice myself to her for a year or two. I want to learn a little bit of what she knows about how to live in this place, how she sees her world.

Several times each day, Doris has come over to me on the boat or out on some island, smiled her wide, transforming smile, said something like "Warm today, eh?" or "Lots of mosquitoes today, eh?" and fallen silent. I've smiled back, responded, "Yes, it's almost hot" or "Yes, it's buggy." And then I've tried to think of something else to say or ask, some way to start a real conversation, each time rendered tongue-tied by several factors—my habitual shyness and reserve and what I suspect might be her own, a reluctance to pry into her life as if I were an ethnographer or a reporter, the vastness of my curiosity and ignorance, the intensity of my desire to know more.

"Do you prefer it to be cold?" I asked one hot afternoon.

"Yes."

Another day I tried, "How long does it take you to skin and butcher a caribou?"

"About an hour."

"How do you do it? Starting with the stomach?"

"Yep."

What I really want to ask is something sweeping and unanswerable, like "What is it like to live your life?" I want to know how she copes with the winter, with the isolation, whether she gets lonely or depressed and if so what she does about it, how she spends her time during the darkest, coldest days. I want to ask if she worries, out alone on her snowmobile, about engine failure or getting lost in a storm or falling through the ice, how she learned to find and track animals, what it feels like to shoot a musk ox or caribou or wolverine, to bury cold hands in warm blood and muscle, whether she runs traplines and snares ptarmigan. I wonder if she has ever learned how to make a traditional igloo, how she keeps her house warm, what she eats all winter and how it is prepared. I want to know exactly how she balances independence and human ties, solitude and loneliness. I have a million questions, maybe more. But I have never managed to ask any of them.

This is likely my last chance to talk to her. I ask her if she remembers how to make any of the string figures we saw Saturday night. She nods. Will you show me some? She nods again and disappears to find a length of string.

Soon she is holding a wolf in her hands. A quick tangle of deft and intricate motions, her fingers bending and twisting, palms swooping together and apart, and now it is a pair of caribou, a hare, two musk oxen. She names each figure as it appears, man in a kayak, fox, loon on a nest, then lets it float for a moment in the space between us, before her hands pull apart and it vanishes.

I watch intently, trying to decipher her movements, see order where it surely is, somewhere in that kaleidoscope of crosses and knots, dropped loops, and flips of the wrist. It seems like magic, the way her hands remember how to move so precisely through a process that looks to me like chaos, the way a simple loop of ordinary kitchen string, arranged just so, can outline a world and a way of seeing. Again and again, a form emerges from nowhere, calls to the imagination, then disappears.

There is something here I want to learn. Doris's string figures somehow embody the impression this place has made on me, how in ways I can't yet begin to articulate, the week I've spent here has been important. So I ask her if she will teach me an easy one. She nods, her hands blur, she holds up an elegant asymmetrical design and says, "Tundra swan."

I laugh. "Something *really* easy," I say. She pauses again, produces a fishing net, and the lesson begins.

When my trip was over and I was back at home living my ordinary life, I thought often about how much I'd learned, and how very little. Once again I had pieced together a story about a place and a few of its inhabitants, a lacy fabric of hints, guesses, and a few magical images. A kind of shadow film kept running in my head, flickering apparitions of summer and then, more faintly, of the coming winter—caribou and musk oxen huddled against the wind, a sleeping bear, Jack with his dog team and Doris on her snowmobile, the sun a garnet glow in the south, the silver moon floating against a field of bright stars.

One day, as I was leafing through a book called *The Poetics of Reverie* by the philosopher Gaston Bachelard, I discovered a passage that spoke straight to me, as if I were its only true reader. In this passage, Bachelard is speculating about the different ways we might find to *be* in the world. Some people, he says, are *world thinkers,* those who reconstruct a world by retracing a long path of reflections. Before the openings of the world, they make it a rule to hesitate. I recognized myself in these words, how I have tried so hard to think about geology and evolution and extinction, the way I reconstructed the hidden worlds of the Pajarito Plateau and Trail Ridge, the doubts that have darkened my vision.

But other people, Bachelard continues, are *world dreamers.* Certain images have the power to cut us loose from ordinary tethers and cast us into reverie. Then, he says, the dreamer "feels a being opening within him. Suddenly such a dreamer is a *world dreamer.* He opens himself to the world, and the world opens itself to him." Again: "When the dreamer is truly the author of his solitude, reverie gives him the impression of a home in the imagined universe." Finally, he asks, "Is it *knowing* to contemplate while dreaming? Is it *understanding?* It is certainly not *perceiving.* The eye which dreams does not see, or at least it sees with another vision." Here, too, I recognized myself, the self that had emerged during my days in the Arctic.

And I mused often about an old photograph I'd seen on the cover of a book at the lodge: an igloo lit from within and glowing a rich sapphire blue against the black night. Everything inside was hidden from view. Nothing was visible of the people who lived there, the effort they had spent to arrive at this spot, to build this house that would last a few weeks at most, to kill the animals whose skins and fat provided the warmth and illumination, to light the lamp and tend the wick, to feed the dogs, mend the clothes, simply to stay alive. Nothing showed of their passions and desires, their loneliness and despair, none of their stories or songs or games, nothing of their stores of resilience and joy.

While the photographer struggled outside in the cold with film and exposures and tripods, inside, I imagine, a family might have been dancing or singing or drumming. The new young priest might have come to visit. An old man tells stories while children play on a rope hung from the ceiling. Caribou cooks in melted snow over a soapstone lamp, with its long cotton-grass wick and pool of seal blubber fuel. An old woman sits mending clothing, chewing on the leather to keep it soft, patching holes made by sharp ice. Now and then she tends the wick, adding a bit of the cotton grass she carries in two tiny bags her mother had made for her long ago, one from the lining of a polar bear's heart, the other from the webbed feet of a red-throated loon.

A young woman sits quietly to one side, her black hair gleaming in the soft light. Perhaps she is dreaming of hunting, of caribou splashing through summer's warm water, the rifle she might someday own. Maybe, years later, she will be Doris's grandmother. Now she holds a long, thin piece of sinew, tied in a loop. Only on the darkest days of the year is she permitted to play these games or teach them to the children. Her hands move, deftly, intricately, and out of nothing appears a caribou, a musk ox, a loon on a nest, a white wolf in the midnight sun.

IV

The World Is a Nest

I lie on my back in the dark, spinning through space with the whole Earth under my spine. John and I are sleeping outside in our yard this cold November night so we can see the Leonid meteor shower, which is predicted to be unusually spectacular. Weasel has burrowed to a spot between our feet (our sleeping bags zip together) and apparently has no intention of moving until morning. Marmot, who is clearly excited by this novel situation, keeps wandering off to rustle in dry leaves, issue soft *ruffs,* and investigate the smells of the night. The thin cloud cover is supposed to blow east before the show gets really intense, sometime around three in the morning.

I've set an alarm next to my head, but I can't get to sleep. I'm chilly, too lazy to go inside for more clothes, and a little worried that the sky won't clear. When I do doze off, Marmot wakes me up. Once in a while, maybe for reassurance and maybe just to be companionable, he swings by to place his icy nose against mine, dip into the sleeping bag by my left arm, turn around a couple of times, then emerge and resume his explorations. I guess the truth is that I'm just as excited as he is.

This small ridge is my home. Here the Rockies rise out of the Great Plains. Bison, woolly mammoths, and dinosaurs have wandered here. The sandstone beneath me was once another mountain range. For a very long time, the stone below the sandstone drifted south of the equator, floating on hidden currents of liquid rock. It has held swamps, ice sheets, steppes, warm inland seas; it has nourished lives beyond counting. One October, a familiar sound caught my ear: sandhill cranes high overhead, nearly a hundred of them, so far up I could see only their shapes. As they may have done for sixty million years, they moved south in a single long, unwavering wedge. I think about how their strong wings stitch the continent together, how they call from the deep past to the present moment, and I drift in and out of sleep.

A few hours later, the clouds disappear and the sky fills with shooting stars. Hundreds of them, sometimes several at once, short streaks of light, long strands of lingering fire, bits of the cosmos come to Earth. Each meteor appears out of emptiness, hangs for an instant in the space above me, then vanishes.

Beneath my spine, worlds weave through worlds, tangled, laced, and layered, seen and unseen, sinew and string, twigs and feathers and spiderweb, delicate strong balls carved of rock, bone, fire, and ice, intricate past all comprehension. Once I read these words: "For the world is a nest, and an immense power holds the inhabitants of the world in this nest." What is this power? What kind of magnetism or gravity? What fierce and tender mixture of kinship and compassion, imagination and love?

My ordinary life passes here at home. Day by day, season by season, I cook, clean my house, take walks with my friends. I try hard to be a good daughter, sister, aunt, wife, and teacher. I scatter mementos around my desk, talismans for a strong spirit—a lichen-splashed musk ox vertebra, a postcard photo of cranes in a morning's mist, a loose stack of dry, papery horsetail segments. I use a slab of stromatolite for a paperweight. I talk with John and play with Marmot and Weasel. A year or so ago, when Weasel started having trouble jumping, I took him to the vet; an X-ray showed arthritis beginning in his spine. The arthritis in my neck continues to bother me, too. One day Marmot climbed onto my desk, ignored a shrink-wrapped strip of musk ox jerky, and ate a tidbit of petrified seal blubber.

After my trip to Bathurst Inlet, I sought out books about that part of the Arctic and found in them echoes of my own preoccupations. The serenity and translucency of the summer light. The wakefulness it engenders, the altered vision. The way the place feels—though is not—timeless. The fortitude, skill, and self-sufficiency of its people. Winter's bitter cold.

Certain details struck me with particular force. Vilhjalmur Stefansson explains that at about the latitude of Bathurst Inlet, even in midwinter when the sun does not rise, at midday it lies only as far beneath the horizon as it would in the Tropics just after sundown. Even on a cloudy winter night, he says, starlight from behind the clouds reflects on the snow, and so the pitch-black nights of lower latitudes are unknown. And Knud Rasmussen repeats what he was told by the Inuit about how the invisible spirits of the air find the proper human bodies to enter. Ordinary people "are like houses with extinguished lamps: they are dark inside and do not attract the attention of the spirits." But the spirits "saw the shamans in the form of shining bodies that attracted and drew them and made them wish to go and live in them and give them their own strength, sight and knowledge." I wondered if I might be underestimating the power of light.

I found several books by the anthropologist Diamond Jenness, who from 1913 to 1918 traveled with the people of the Arctic coast. I lived in his diary for a week—all eight hundred pages of it including footnotes. The foreword describes that part of the Far North as being "at the edge of imagination." And I spent a long time studying Jenness's collection of string figures. Most of them are incredibly complex, beautiful and cryptic. I tried to learn some of the simpler shapes, two brown bears, two caribou with their antlers. His descriptions sound so detailed, his vocabulary so precise: *distal* and *proximal* and *palmar* and *transverse*. But I couldn't crack the code, and all I could make was knots. It was in Jenness's book I learned that these games were taboo except on days the sun didn't rise, and I remembered how quickly Doris said she'd forgotten how to make the figure of a bear.

I followed other threads. With instructions and a map from Jim Benedict, John and I found the stone game drive on Trail Ridge, where people hunted four and a half millennia ago. I learned more than I wanted to know about Rocky Flats, the nuclear weapons plant just upwind from where I grew up, one of the most toxic places anywhere. I found more ptarmigan on Poetry Curve. I took several more field seminars—on winter adaptations of small mammals, on lichens. On another short trip to Canada, I drove to see the Burgess Shale, the source of those wildly imaginative hard-bodied creatures I'd read about and drawn on my time line. Some 525 million years ago, they lived near the equator in a warm ocean; now their fossils rest on a steep mountainside in the Rockies, far inland and nearly 10,000 feet high. Nearly everything I read addressed the questions I'd been researching, and I collected a thick file of newspaper and magazine clippings.

Sometimes it seemed the world was shaping itself to my obsessions. On the Pajarito Plateau, a prescribed fire escaped control, and 48,000 acres of ponderosas and junipers burned. Truckloads of soil were removed from the edge of Los Alamos Canyon: with the groundcover gone, late-summer floods might release those early radioactive wastes. A few weeks later, a car crash ignited another wildfire in the grasslands of eastern Washington, at the Hanford Nuclear Reservation, a place built to turn uranium into plutonium. Among the 190,000 acres that burned were the sites of three old radioactive waste dumps.

On a good day in the first new diamond mine to open in Canada's Northwest Territories, 900,000 tons of rocks were shoveled from open pits under drained lakes in the tundra, trucked, crushed, scrubbed, ground, spun, and X-rayed to yield a coffee can full of high-quality jewels. Just a few miles from my home, a crew digging sewers unearthed the skull and tusks of a woolly mammoth, 15 or 20 thousand years old. A man walked through our campsite in southern Colorado after breakfast one morning, and we struck up a conversation. He was another marmot biologist checking the subalpine colonies he'd been monitoring for nearly four decades; I recognized his name from the reading I'd done. Like ptarmigan, he told me, marmots eat flowers. They like columbines and cow parsnip, and they love dandelions so much that you can map their foraging territories by the absence of these blossoms.

There is always some dark news to plunge me into grief. Another cousin dies, and an uncle; my brother falls gravely ill but slowly recovers; several good friends encounter mortal danger. One autumn I hear on the radio about the nearly certain extinction of Miss Waldron's red colobus monkey, a large primate that until not long ago played in big noisy groups in the treetops of the West African rainforest. I spend a few days at the library trying without much success to learn more about the character and lives of these animals. The *colobus* in their name refers to their short or absent thumbs. Unlike other colobus monkeys, they were patrilineal, but they were also less concerned with hierarchies, dominance, and conflict than others. They were victims, most directly, of the bush-meat trade, which means that they were hunted to extinction for food. The next autumn's disaster is more much dramatic, faster, and highly visible: the violent deaths of September 11 and the war that followed. A voice in my head says over and over, *We live in the Age of Loneliness.*

I think often about a story I heard not long ago, a Buddhist parable: A child is drowning in a lake. The child's mother watches from the shore, but she has no arms and no legs, and nobody hears her cries. She can do nothing to save her child from suffering. What she feels is what Buddhists call compassion.

Yet the world is also lit by beauty and grace. I want to appreciate every gift without holding anything back, love every particle of good, absorb it all, seize those bits of joy and hold on to them tightly. I spend more time now with my friends. I give parties to mark the coming of winter and the shortest day; I string more colored lights against the darkness; I try never to miss a meteor shower or a full moon. I watch the sky more often, hang more bird feeders, study the deer that browse on our trees.

Darkness and light. They whirl together until they blur, they layer into convoluted whorls. One afternoon in the Far North, two caribou spin in a tight circle, one pale in winter's coat, one dark in summer's. This is not just a metaphor. I study a piece of stromatolite the size of my palm: shades of brown, tiny patches of lichen, a miniature landscape of plateaus and shadowed canyons. In fact it looks remarkably like the model of the Pajarito Plateau in a visitor center near Los Alamos, though these shapes seem a little more convoluted, chaotic. No straight lines, rough to my touch. Here and there a tiny grain glitters in the light of my desk lamp. Life and death in equal portions, breathing bodies become stone. This is not a metaphor, either, but a fact.

*T*wo years ago in April, a group of Tibetan monks came to my campus for a week. They would build from colored grains of sand a mandala for the healing of the world.

On Tuesday morning I went to a lecture about the meaning of the ceremony. I was curious, partly because in China years before, on the high Tibetan Plateau, I'd watched a sand mandala being constructed in an old Buddhist monastery, one that had somehow survived the Cultural Revolution, though I'd read recently that the Chinese might be closing it now. John and I were teaching in a neighboring province, and our school had brought us for a visit; at the time, this place was far off the tourist path, and Tibet itself was still closed to all travelers, so I felt very lucky to be there.

It was April then, too, and cold. Snow fell on and off the two days we stayed, and everyone wore many layers of clothes.

A few Chinese tourists laughed and took photos of each other in theatrical poses. Monks were everywhere, maroon-robed, hair cropped short. Pilgrims wrapped in thick wool inched their way towards the temples, measuring the ground with their prostrate bodies, then walked around buildings spinning prayer wheels and making offerings of silk scarves and yak hair pasted with yak butter to stone walls and altars. In the late afternoon, we watched a class of boys sitting in a wide arc on the ground, chanting, shouting and clapping in theological debates, waving giant ceremonial hats that looked like fringed yellow moons. The many buildings flickered with the dim light of yak butter lamps. Decorations filled every surface and space—tapestries and paintings, banners and flags, elaborately painted eaves and columns, carved golden Buddhas, intricate sculptures of dyed yak butter, gods and goddesses and strange spirits, the fantastic figures of dreams.

On the balconies of one small courtyard stood a row of animals, stuffed and glass-eyed, draped with scarves, a horse, a bear, some animals I didn't recognize. One, I learned much later, was a takin, the closest relative of the musk ox. In another larger courtyard, old men bent low over their mandala, laying down thin trickles of sand according to patterns that were twenty-five hundred years old. They worked with infinite care, and a universe emerged beneath their patient hands. I understood little of what I was seeing, though, and nothing of what I heard.

Now was my chance to learn a little more, this time right at home in the student center on campus, one of the buildings whose basement had been badly damaged by the Spring Creek flood.

A young monk translated the words of the eldest. They

spoke simply for an audience of beginners. We teach with good intentions, they began, as a kind of giving, which is one of the virtues. There are two mandalas, an inner, the more important, and an outer, where understanding must begin. The outer mandala may be carved of wood, painted on cloth, or assembled from some kind of powder. Wood makes clear how a mandala is a house, the palace or residence of an enlightened being. Powders such as sand have three virtues. Many grains earn extra merit. Each grain takes on the blessings and healing energies of the whole, so when the mandala is finished, we can share its medicine with the invisible spirits who are everywhere around us and who make every place sacred. And because it is hard to make but easy to dismantle, a sand mandala reveals the nature of impermanence.

They spoke of good heart and of emptiness. One begins by renouncing self-cherishing. One must control one's own bad emotions, prevent them from continuing. Thus one frees oneself from suffering. Then one strives for compassion, for universal love, willing all other beings to be free from suffering. Finally one may attain the wisdom of emptiness. Emptiness, the monks explained, is a difficult and dangerous idea. Misunderstood as nothingness, it leads to nihilism. It requires intensive study and much effort. We *are* here, we *exist*, we feel things.

"Is there a necessary link between compassion and emptiness?" someone asked. The small room was nearly full, and many people were taking notes, as I was.

"Yes," they answered. Ignorance leads to self-cherishing, but the wisdom of emptiness destroys ignorance. The older man paused, then tried to explain again. Things exist, but not inherently, in themselves, from inside, because things are not separate.

"What is my self?" asked someone else.

We must go deeper; the problem gets harder. The self can't be separated. Things exist only in appearance. And in conceptualization. Still we exist. But our existence depends on something. Hence one's own happiness and the happiness of others depend on each other.

The mandala they were beginning downstairs, the monks said, was a particularly powerful one, especially good for times when bad things happen. It was the residence for a female Buddha who would sit in the star at its center. It would heal even those who only looked at it.

I walked outside beneath the sweet pink blossoms of a crabapple, got in my car, and drove home. What a powerful philosophy this was, I thought: to face suffering and renounce it, to contemplate emptiness and practice compassion, to refuse nihilism but embrace transience. For these men it was also a culture and a faith, a culture being pushed towards extinction, a faith I wished I could share.

I made a sandwich and turned on the radio to hear the noon forecast; I'd heard snow might be coming. Something dreadful was happening, though no one yet knew exactly what, and even the basic story would be hours in coming. Not far to the south, two boys had walked into their high school and started killing their classmates. Their first shots, I realized later, had come with the monks' closing chant, or perhaps a few minutes later as I paused outside to breathe in the scent of spring.

On Thursday evening, two days later, the monks gave a performance of traditional songs and chants to a packed auditorium. At its end, the young monk spoke briefly. "We are very sorry for this tragedy," he said, "and now we would like to offer a prayer of purification and healing for the families and community." Seven men stood in a line across the stage, robed in maroon, each with his head and one shoulder bare, eyes closed, hands empty. They started low, chanting, and then, after a long while, they rose into melody, sung out high and full. Their bodies swayed slightly. I had no idea what words they sang, but as I had done all week, I kept thinking, beyond all reason, that I was not quite but almost hearing a word I did know. "Joy joy joy," they seemed to chant. "Joy joy joy joy joy."

The next day the mandala was finished. Though I'd come early for the closing ceremony, the room was jammed, and I had to pick my way to a perch high on a platform in a corner, not far from the center of activity. I saw many of my friends, and John was there, too, though I couldn't see him in the crowd. The monks began with music—horns, a drum, cymbals, bell, shaker. A big man cupped his hand in front of his mouth and brought music from deep in his throat. The rest chanted and sang quietly, standing in a line behind the sturdy table.

The mandala was beautiful, brightly colored, symmetrical, elaborate. It offered no answers, no explanations; it solved nothing; it only represented. Yet like Doris's string figures, it seemed to me dense with the meanings of life. One ring repeated the signs of the visible world: a tree, a swan, a person, a bone.

Suddenly, with a small brass tool, the eldest monk began to scrape the sand into the center, first from the west, then south, east, north. His hands moved quickly. With an ordinary plastic dust brush, a second monk swept more sand to the center in lines that swirled the way fire swirls around a spinning body. The pattern vanished into a blur of colors. The pile grew until finally two men scooped it with their hands into a lidded jar, careful to collect every blessed and healing grain.

In a few minutes, they'd fill small glass vials to give to anyone who waited. The rest of the sand would go to Spring Creek, where the monks would sprinkle it on moving water, to heal the invisible spirits who are everywhere. First, though, they covered the jar with a brocade hood, sang some more, played more music. Then they nodded and smiled. The ceremony was over.

*I*t's been almost six years since I lay in the winter sun on the Pajarito Plateau and listened to a long filament of cranes moving north into spring. Sometimes I ask myself what in all this time I've learned—from so much reading, from moving around the land in search of something I could barely name, all that solitary brooding. Have I realized anything new and important? Or have I seen only what I should always have known?

The earth is old. Nothing lasts. All life is kin. Different eyes perceive different worlds, and much remains hidden. Ours is an age of extinctions; ours are the hands of the destroyers. Grief and beauty are knotted together. Curiosity and imagination are fundamental human forces. So are fear and hatred, passion and compassion. None of this is surprising.

But scale matters. At this high level of generality, everything seems obvious. When I focus on smaller things, the picture changes. Horsetails have been around for four hundred million years, cranes maybe sixty million. One uranium isotope that is involved in nuclear chain reactions has a half-life of seven hundred million years. About every two weeks all winter long, yellow-bellied marmots arouse themselves from hibernation. Lichens absorb radionuclides. White-tailed ptarmigan have feathered eyelids and eat flower blossoms. On summer days in the Arctic, loons with bloodred throats guard their nests. Some people know how to create a wolf out of string. Miss Waldron's red colobus monkeys have all died; *kolobos* is the Greek word for mutilated. The lines on a chunk of rock more than a billion years old match the swirls on my fingertips. The world is made of details.

Still my questions are sweeping and unanswerable; they make my head spin. When I may never know a person as old as a century, what sense is there in the immense age of the stone underfoot, what blend of comfort and grief? What is it to speak of a particular place, to name it timeless, lovely, or spare, to love or desire it? Or what we call life: What kinship ties me to a crane, a ptarmigan, a chunk of fossilized cyanobacteria? A wolf or a seismosaurus, dead and buried, its bones scrubbed clean? What *is* this Earth? What are we all doing here? How shall I think about my life?

I play with words, big words: *creation* and *extinction, despair* and *beauty, bodies* and *spirits, loneliness* and *compassion.* I use them as though I knew what they meant, as though a pair of words could explain a paradox, but I find only glimpses of what might be understanding, images that flicker and vanish when I look at them directly.

Once in a while, I think maybe I manage to think and dream in the same instant. I understand better now how hard it is to cultivate balance, and how crucial. I have always wanted to direct my attention and my actions outwards, into the material world; I have learned that I must also tend to my spirit.

Lately I've been thinking a lot about this word *spirit,* and especially about the concept of invisible spirits. Knud Rasmussen heard about them from the Inuit: the invisible spirits of the air, who could enter the shining bodies of the shamans and give them their strength, sight, and knowledge. The Tibetan monks spoke of how such spirits are everywhere around us, making every place sacred. I have trouble making concrete sense of these statements; they're too vague, too unverifiable, too immaterial, too distant from my own sense of what counts as real. Yet something about this notion has taken root in my imagination. I want very much to think of invisible spirits not as an item of faith, not even as a powerful metaphor, but as a plain *fact*.

I remember one evening during that spring of sadness. I'd been sagging in front of the television, overwhelmed by the usual bad news. "You need to get out of the house," John said, clicking off the set midword. "Let's take the pupsters into town for a walk along the river."

Twenty minutes later we'd set off along the Cache La Poudre River, switching from the paved bike path to the dirt track alongside at the will of the dogs, who pulled us everywhere with sniffing excitement, heads down and tails up. Clumps of weeds, a grasshopper, a buffet of varied and evidently fine manures, a passing cyclist—it all fascinated them. My knee was hurting, though, so I sent John and the dogs ahead and found a chair-sized rock to sit on.

I looked around me. The river was muddy, its banks a mess of rough-barked cottonwoods, mashed grasses and weeds, flood debris, churned-up mud. To the north, the raw desolation of a gravel quarry. To the south, sagging barbed wire, weedy brown pasture. It was an unprepossessing scene, familiar and banal.

The late sun was nice, though, warm and golden, with a bit of color in the sky over the mountains. And John had left with me our new pair of binoculars—nothing fancy, but a step up for us. So I started my usual inefficient routine: find something to look at, take my glasses off, bring the binos to my eyes, point in what I hope is the right direction, fiddle with the focus. A rusty, twisted barb on the fence, sharp against a field of tan fuzz. Cottonwood bark transformed into a landscape of shadowed canyons. Sharp-edged spikes of needle-and-thread grass catching some stray glints of light. A flock of swallows zipping across my field of vision, not quite in focus.

Just above the path to the west hovered a vague cloud of bugs, made visible by the sun behind them. I aimed towards the sun, shifted my angle until the glare disappeared, and brought the swarm into focus.

It was the most amazing vision. They looked like small moths, and I suppose there might have been a couple hundred of them. Some hovered in place as hummingbirds hover at feeders, moving in quick jerks, each one a clear circular blur of beating wings. But it was the others that surprised me so much. They looked like long, twisted ribbons, like sparkling streamers on New Year's Eve, each one a spinning helix of energy made visible. They floated up and down and sideways; they caught and held the light of the setting sun as if it were their own.

For a few minutes I forgot everything else and simply stared in astonishment. Then I concentrated on memorizing what I was seeing, knowing already that soon enough I might doubt my memory. Was it a quirk of perspective, of focus, something about the angle of the sun or the optics of my new binoculars, some kind of trick? In the intense elation of the moment, I didn't care.

Finally a waft of air moved the cloud of bugs out of my sight.

At home I tried to duplicate the helix shape, cutting strips of paper and scrounging for ribbon scraps, then twisting and twirling them. Yes, those were the forms I'd seen, but the magic was missing. I tried to draw them, too, but failed. Nothing I could make at my kitchen table could be more than the crudest approximation.

Still, I haven't forgotten the marvel of this moment—how in that most ordinary time and place, in the absurd and improbable form of bugs swarming over an asphalt path, I felt for an instant that I was *seeing*.

But what was I seeing? If I were more mystical, I'd probably call it the fire of life itself. Or maybe it was a reminder that joy and beauty can materialize suddenly out of what seems to be empty space. Maybe in this fleeting moment, my self and my place matched perfectly, and so I could see what was truly there, the swirl of energy all around me. Or maybe it was a glimpse beyond concept into fact: nothing more and nothing less than insects spinning and floating above the ground.

Now I wonder this: What if these were some of the invisible spirits of the air, simply revealed to me by a certain slant of light? Invisible because I don't usually see them, not because they have no presence in the material world; spirits because they hold their own place in the creation, cherish their own share of life. And I think about all the other things I've learned to remember are present even when I can't see them. It's such a long list! Radioactive particles and rays, the buried bones and fossils of the past, the motion of the continents. Marmots in hibernation, ptarmigans asleep under the snow. A white wolf in all the unwitnessed hours of its life. I envision Doris out on her snowmobile in the dark of November—but it is not so dark after all, for the moon is full and the aurora flames across the sky.

A year ago, a day or two before Christmas, I was alone in the house and feeling a little sad. So I turned on the colored lights and lit a bit of juniper incense. I found a loop of yarn and practiced making a fishing net. Then I sat on my couch and began to imagine the people I have loved who now are gone, sitting one at a time in the faded blue velvet chair across from me for a short visit. First, because the chair was hers, my father's mother in one of her trademark royal blue suits, broad-brimmed blue felt hats, thick-heeled lace-up shoes. Next was my mother's mother, eager as she always was to tell me what she'd been doing. Then Carol Ann appeared, and my great-grandmothers, cousins and uncles and aunts, lost friends. They sat across from me with the clarity and solidity that once had been theirs, and each one brought a measure of grace. With each visitor, I felt less sad. The room filled up with spirits.

This winter I'll throw a bigger party. I'll summon every spirit I can imagine with any concreteness at all, not only humans but all living creatures, not only the recent dead but the long vanished and we who are still alive. Maybe I'll invite them all to join me on a boat—we'll all fit, since spirits like these don't need much space—and then we'll set out to float for a while on the waters that mirror the sky.

Notes

I looked at many dozens of books and articles in the course of writing this book, far too many to cite in detail. I do want to acknowledge a few, though—the ones I found most useful overall, the origins of the few statements I quoted directly, and a sampling of the more technical sources that have helped me learn about the matters I've been exploring. I tried to be careful with how I used these sources and checked my facts when I could, but I am sure that I have not managed either to recognize all disputed areas or to avoid all outright errors.

I. The Voice of the Crane

The information in this chapter is from particularly scattered sources. I can, however, point to some highlights.

First I must mention two books I turned to again and again: Audrey DeLella Benedict's *Sierra Club Naturalist's Guide: The Southern Rockies* (San Francisco: Sierra Club Books, 1991) and Richard Cowen's *History of Life*, 2d ed. (Boston: Blackwell Scientific Publications, 1995). Both of these books tell enormous stories with admirable clarity and helped me put my fragments of information together into a coherent picture.

On evolution, I found another helpful overview in Thomas N. Taylor and Edith L. Taylor's *Biology and Evolution of Fossil Plants* (Englewood Cliffs, N.J.: Prentice-Hall, 1993). Daniel Axelrod's article "Cenozoic History of Some Western American Pines," *Annals of the Missouri Botanical Garden* 73, no. 3 [1986]: 565–641, was quite helpful. *The Natural History of Squirrels* was written by John Gurnell (New York and Oxford: Facts on File Publications, 1987). One of several good sources on sandhill cranes is the entry by T. C. Tacha, S. A. Nesbitt, and P. A. Vohs in *The Birds of North America,* no. 31, ed. A. Poose, P. Stettenheim, and F. Gill (Philadelphia: Academy of Natural Sciences; Washington, D.C.: American Ornithologists' Union, 1992). I found some details about the Cambrian Explosion fossils in Wayne Powell's *Geoscience Guide to the Burgess Shale: Geology and Paleontology in Yoho National Park,* 2d ed. (Field, B.C.: Yoho–Burgess Shale Foundation, 1997).

On geology, I looked at Halka Chronic's *Roadside Geology of New Mexico* (Missoula: Mountain Press Publishing, 1987), and I found a good set of maps of continental drift in Anthony Hallam's *Outline of Phanerozoic Biogeography,* Oxford Biogeography Series, no. 10 (Oxford: Oxford University Press, 1994). Jeff Eighmy, a colleague at Colorado State University who works with archaeomagnetic dating, helped me understand magnetism and the reversal of Earth's magnetic poles.

I found Charles Darwin's quotation from Charles Lyell in *The Origin of Species,* ed. Gillian Beer (Oxford: Oxford University Press, 1996), p. 251.

On Los Alamos, nuclear bombs, and radioactive waste, several sources were important. Richard Rhodes's phrase about

Emperor Hirohito's voice is from *The Making of the Atomic Bomb* (New York: Simon and Schuster, 1986), p. 745. Mari Asano told me about the implications of this phrase. The quotations about the Trinity test and Truman's comment about the bombing of Hiroshima came from *Los Alamos: Beginning of an Era, 1943–1945* (reprint, Los Alamos: Los Alamos Historical Society, 1986).

The citizen watchdog group I visited in Santa Fe was the Los Alamos Study Group, and the government document they sent me to in the Los Alamos National Laboratory Public Reading Room was LA-6848-MS, vol. 1, "History and Environmental Setting of LASL Near-Surface Land Disposal Facilities for Radioactive Wastes (Areas A, B, C, D, E, F, G, and T)," by Margaret Anne Rogers (Los Alamos: Los Alamos Scientific Laboratory, June 1997). I found most of my information on half-lives on a Web site written by Mark Winter of the University of Sheffield, England, at http://www.shef.ac.uk/chemistry/web-elements/fr-radio/periodic-table.html (1993–1998); I also consulted a table by James A. Plambeck (1996) at http://c.chem.ualberta.ca/~plambeck/che/data/p00431.htm. I found interesting information in William L. Graf's *Plutonium and the Rio Grande: Environmental Change and Contamination in the Nuclear Age* (New York: Oxford University Press, 1994).

II. The Edge of Winter

My immunologist (and writer) friend is Gerald Callahan, and it was he who first told me about the research suggesting that we have light sensors in the backs of our knees. See S. S. Campbell and P. J. Murphy, "Extraocular Circadian Phototransduction in Humans," *Science* 279, no. 5349 [January 16, 1998]: 396–99.

Audrey Benedict's guide to the southern Rockies was helpful here again, as were Halka Chronic's *Roadside Geology of Colorado* (Missoula: Mountain Press Publishing, 1980) and Ann H. Zwinger and Beatrice E. Willard's *Land Above the Trees: A Guide to American Alpine Tundra* (New York: Harper and Row, 1972; reprint, Boulder: Johnson Books, 1996). I found out just how windy it gets on Trail Ridge in D. E. Glidden's *Winter Wind Studies in Rocky Mountain National Park* (Estes Park, Colo.: Rocky Mountain Nature Association, 1982).

To better understand winter ecology, I looked at several collections of scientific papers, such as Cynthia Carey, Gregory L. Florant, Bruce A. Wunder, and Barbara Horwitz, eds., *Life in the Cold: Ecological, Physiological, and Molecular Mechanisms* (Boulder: Westview Press, 1993), and at two good general introductions, James C. Halfpenny and Roy Douglas Ozanne's *Winter: An Ecological Handbook* (Boulder: Johnson Books, 1989) and Peter J. Marchand's *Life in the Cold: An Introduction to Winter Ecology,* 3d ed. (Hanover, N.H.: University Press of New England, 1996).

The line about lichens being organisms united in adversity comes from David L. Hawksworth and Francis Rose's *Lichens As Pollution Monitors,* Institute of Biology's Studies in Biology, no. 66 (London: Edward Arnold, 1976), p. 7. Another good overview of lichens is William Purvis, *Lichens* (Washington, D.C.: Smithsonian Institution Press; London: Natural History Museum, 2000); this is where I read about the experiment involving lichen tolerance of radioactivity and about the lethal human dose.

Ken Giesen and Greg Florant were not the only biologists from whom I learned about the tundra. Among the teachers of the other field seminars I took at Rocky Mountain National Park were Bruce Wunder (on winter adaptations of small mammals), Beatrice Willard (on tundra flowers), and Roger Rosentreter and Ann Debolt (on lichens). The seminar program is run by the Rocky Mountain Nature Association, P.O. Box 3100, Estes Park, CO 80517.

The poem by Theodore Roethke is called "The Waking"; it may be found in *The Collected Poems of Theodore Roethke* (Garden City, N.Y.: Doubleday, Anchor Press, 1975), p. 104.

III. String Games

I referred to an excellent geology handout written by Bathurst Inlet Lodge naturalist Page Burt; much of my other information came from the evening slide-show talks by Glenn and Trish Warner, Jack Sperry, and Page.

The passages about world thinking and world dreaming come from Gaston Bachelard's *The Poetics of Reverie: Childhood, Language, and the Cosmos*, trans. Daniel Russell (Boston: Beacon Press, 1971), pp. 173–78.

The photograph of the glowing igloo is on the dust jacket of Fred Bruemmer's book of photos, many of them from Bathurst Inlet, *Seasons of the Eskimo: A Vanishing Way of Life* (Greenwich, Conn.: New York Graphic Society, 1971). I have not been able to confirm my memory of the color of this image, since the copy of the book I found through interlibrary loan had no jacket.

IV. The World Is a Nest

The line about the world being a nest is from Gaston Bachelard's *Poetics of Space*, trans. Maria Jolas (Boston: Beacon Press, 1969), p. 104.

The books about the Arctic I mention most specifically here are Vilhjalmur Stefansson's *Hunters of the Great North*

(New York: Harcourt, Brace, 1922) (see p. 115 on the lack of absolute darkness); Knud Rasmussen's *Intellectual Culture of the Copper Eskimos: Report of the Fifth Thule Expedition, 1921–24,* vol. 9 (Copenhagen: Gyldendalske Boghandel, Nordisk Forlag, 1932; reprint, New York: AMS, 1976) (for spirits and shamans, see p. 28); *Arctic Odyssey: The Diary of Diamond Jenness, Ethnologist with the Canadian Arctic Expedition in Northern Alaska and Canada, 1913–1916,* ed. Stuart E. Jenness (Hull, Quebec: Canadian Museum of Civilization, 1991) (this is where I learned that women sometimes carried cotton-grass seeds in bags made from the webbed feet of loons and the membranes lining the hearts of polar bears; see p. 813); and Diamond Jenness, *Report of the Canadian Arctic Expedition 1913–18, Volume XIII: Eskimo Folk-Lore, Part B: Eskimo String Figures* (Ottawa: F. A. Acland, 1924).

The book that guided me to the game drive on Trail Ridge was James B. Benedict's *Game Drives of Rocky Mountain National Park,* Research Report no. 7 (Ward, Colo.: Center for Mountain Archeology, 1996). Jim, who sent me other useful materials as well, also first told me about Diamond Jenness.

Acknowledgments

*T*hinking about the many friends who have helped me through the often lonely process of living and writing this book, I'm filled with warmth. My first thanks must go to my husband, John Calderazzo, who gave me all kinds of support, not the least of which was reading and talking with me about the manuscript many times.

I'm very grateful to these valued friends who also responded with encouragement and suggestions to the whole book-in-progress: Chuck Bergman, Nina Bjornsson, Mike Branch, Jonathan Cobb, Pattie Cowell, Sue Doe, Colleen Fullbright, Kaaron Jorgen, Gina Mohr Callahan, Liza Nelligan, and Sherry Pomering. Jim Benedict, Gerry Callahan, Valerie Cohen, David Mogen, and Emilie Buchwald commented on parts of the manuscript; Greg Florant, Ken Giesen, Cynthia Melcher, and Bruce Wunder helped with fact checking. Dawn Marano, my fine editor, gave me excellent advice.

Many others—so many I can't name them all here, I'm both

sorry and happy to say—have encouraged me in other important ways. Warm thanks to all of you. And thanks to Mary Lea Dodd; to my parents, Laird and Nancy Campbell; and (though they'll never read this page) to Marmot and Weasel.

About the Author

SueEllen Campbell is professor of English at Colorado State University and the author of *Bringing the Mountain Home*. She lives in Bellvue, Colorado. (Photograph by Stephanie G'Schwind.)